PRAISE FOR THE AHA! HANDBOOK

Donna Hartney brilliantly bucks the conventional wisdom that "life-altering AHA!s are as rare as they are powerful" with 21 epiphany-encouraging actions to help us deepen the frequency with which we find meaning in the ups and downs of our lives. With a strong performance consulting and research background, Hartney walks us all down a path to spark more transforming realizations in our lives. She has a gift for seamlessly weaving together stories, research, advice and reflection questions to demonstrate that pivotal realizations are available to all of us—right under the ground we're already walking on, should we choose to look.

JENNY BLAKE, Author of *Life After College: The Complete Guide to Getting What You Want*

It seemed counter-intuitive to me that you could, with intention, spark life-changing epiphanies. However, after reading the first few chapters I began to see the simplicity in what The AHA! Handbook is suggesting. The real-life examples were very helpful, and reading about famous people whose lives you are aware of really helped to illustrate the points without making it seem like "science." I really enjoyed the book. I can't wait until it hits the bookshelves, as I will be recommending it highly to many people in my life.

MACHELLE WILLIAMS, General Manager of Organizational Development and Diversity, Volkswagen Group of America

I've witnessed the incredible impact that flashes of insight can have on people's careers—whether they're workplace superstars or employees at risk. The challenge has always been that career-transforming AHA!s have been a hit or miss proposition. Not any more! The AHA! Handbook shows all of us, step-by-step, how to position ourselves for pivotal insights. How cool is that!

DANA CARTER, Global HR leader,
International health care company

Want to take control of your life? Your own life? Donna Hartney writes from a key moment of self-revelation—and then examines dozens of other lives—as she offers all of us an opportunity to grasp those moments of incredible self-insight that can transform our sense of self and our vision of our personal futures. So easily ignored, yet so powerful if embraced. Donna outlines the "why" and the "how." Grab it and accelerate your choice of the right decisions for your life. Self-inspiration is the best inspiration, and Donna shows us how to access and exploit those rare moments that we can so easily forget to notice!!

JOHN MCBRIDE, Ph.D., Partner, McBride&Lucius,
International performance consulting firm

I love The AHA! Handbook! *I can't wait to share it with my patients, people who are living with the realities of diabetes. Every day I try to motivate diabetics to make lifestyle changes to enhance their well-being and overall health. This book lays the groundwork for sparking behavior changes in my patients. It's an easy-to-follow guide that shows all of us how to see the opportunities for change in our lives and to position ourselves for momentous insights.*

BETSEY DECHERT-BOSS, R.N., B.S.N., M.S.N.,
Certified Family Nurse Practitioner, Certified Diabetes Educator

Donna has done it again! First she created xSAIL Coaching, a powerful tool coaches can use to help their clients spark profound AHA!s in their lives and careers. Now she has written The AHA! Handbook, *a book that delivers to every reader the same opportunity to create life-changing insights! Engaging, moving, and inspirational,* The AHA! Handbook *is a must-read for anyone who wants to reach higher.*

ROSANNE DEE, President, RT Dee and Associates, Inc.,
Certified xSAIL Coach

THE AHA! HANDBOOK

HOW TO SPARK THE INSIGHTS THAT WILL TRANSFORM YOUR LIFE AND CAREER

THE

AHA!

HANDBOOK

HOW TO SPARK THE INSIGHTS
THAT WILL TRANSFORM YOUR
LIFE AND CAREER

DONNA HARTNEY, PH.D.

SFP

FRANKLIN STREET PRESS

Design by Cindy Kiple
ISBN: 978-0-982-13281-4

Franklin Street Press
3959 North Buffalo Street
Orchard Park, New York 14127
info@donnahartney.com
www.donnahartney .com

Manufactured in the United States of America

To David
and
In memory of Nell

Contents

During a recent speech I asked the audience three questions.

"Have you ever had an insight—a flash of clarity that answered a question, solved a problem, or ignited a creative idea?" Everyone in the room raised a hand.

Then I asked, "Have you ever had an insight that made you a different person, a better person, or a more successful person, because it transformed your career, your health, your relationships, your spiritual life, or your commitment to making a difference in the world?" Most of the people in the audience lifted their hands again.

Finally I asked, "Do you know what you can do, the steps you can take, to create the kind of insights that will transform your life?" One person held up a hand.

My mission is a simple one. I want to pose each of those questions and have every person raise a hand with confidence and certainty every time.

Donna Hartney
June 9, 2012

Getting to AHA!

The jolt of an insight. The elation of an epiphany. The flash of an aha. Most of us have them from time to time. But not all ahas are created equally. This book is about a special kind of aha—something I call an AHA!. Let me explain.

The experience of an aha is a fairly common one. It's that sudden flash of clarity that answers a question, solves a problem, or ignites a creative idea. An aha usually arrives when we've puzzled over something for a while and then moved on to something else. Then out of the blue the aha bursts into being. I experience ahas quite a lot. Perhaps you do too. I've had ahas, for example, that revealed to me the missing word in a crossword puzzle, that gave me just the right words for a difficult conversation, or that showed me how I could structure a solution for a business client.

> *This book is about a special kind of aha— something I call an AHA!*

While ordinary ahas can be extremely helpful, they are not the focus of this book. This book focuses on AHA!s. AHA!s are the kind of insights that have a very personal and profound impact on the person who experienced it. In a flash of clarity, the person sees the world differently and is forever changed. It is a defining moment that transforms a person's health, relationships, career, spiritual life, or commitment to making a real difference in the world.

I was lucky enough to experience an AHA! in 1984. It caught me off guard and solved a dilemma that I had been struggling with for several years. In a sudden flash of clarity I understood why I wasn't happy in my career. I was trying to shoehorn myself into a career that wasn't a fit for me! And if I continued to limit my options, I foresaw that I'd be twenty-something, burned out, and of no use to myself or anyone. In that moment I made a decision to go down a different path. That AHA! didn't show me what career would be a good fit for me. It would take time for me to figure that out. The gift that I received that day was the freedom to look.

When it comes to AHA!s we're at the mercy of fate, luck, and chance. Or are we?

We know quite a bit about how to prime ourselves for ordinary ahas. Frame the problem. Investigate the situation. Pose a question and put it on the back burner to simmer. Then, wait. Unfortunately, we can't say the same about what it takes to spark AHA!s. When it comes to life-changing AHA!s we're at the mercy of fate, luck, and chance. Or are we?

MY PATH TO AHA!

I have a tendency to get in my own way in life, and sometimes the usual tactics of thinking things through, applying willpower, or trying to learn from experience just don't help. Thankfully, I also know how to generate transformational AHA!s. But that hasn't always been the case.

In 1994 I earned my Ph.D. but I also hit a wall. I enjoyed my work as a performance consultant but found myself asking, "Now what?" I took some time off to figure things out. I joked with my family and friends that I was *practicing* retirement. I continued to struggle. As I dug deeper, I saw that I wouldn't be able to find clarity until I had managed to deal with my underlying sense of fear and uncertainty. So I set on a path of self-improvement and self-help. I read books, attended classes, and took a close-up look at the defining experiences of my life. Eventually I went back to work as a performance consultant, helping business clients develop effective strategies to bring out the best in people. But I continued to search for answers.

A few years later my husband and I moved into a new house and set aside a weekend to paint the basement. I was looking forward to it—a mindless task perfect for unwinding and letting my thoughts wander. As we painted, though, I noticed the turmoil in my mind. Instead of relaxing I was constantly monitoring my thoughts to identify any that were out of line and then to act quickly to sync them with the self-improvement principles I had been studying. My efforts to move forward had actually made things worse.

In the weeks and months that followed, I focused on finding self-improvement ideas and approaches that netted results for me, and throwing out those that didn't. Eventually I was left with just two concepts. The first one was to recognize when I'd fallen into a pit of unproductive feelings and to not try to think my way out of it. Rather, I should focus on being in the moment, knowing that I'd eventually come out of the abyss. The second idea was that while I was in an emotional hole I might experience an insight and begin to see things differently. Then I wouldn't fall into that same pit again.

Focusing on the two concepts helped. When I was hit with unpleasant emotions, I would no longer try to talk myself out of them. Instead I'd notice them and wait patiently for them to dissipate. And I'd hope to have an insight that would uncover and eliminate the root cause of the emotion. I was finally making progress in my life. Before long I began to wonder whether there was a way to be more proactive. Could I prime myself for pivotal AHA!s rather than just waiting for them to appear?

That's when I found myself in uncharted territory. As a Ph.D. performance consultant my natural inclination was to turn to the research to see what had been studied before. But I could not find a research-based approach to generating life-changing insights. I dug into related areas such as creativity, innovation, and neuroscience.

As I read, I also began to experiment with my thinking. I paid attention to how I was "being" in the world—how I was thinking, how I was feeling, how I was seeing things. I noticed how I was getting in my own way—my thoughts that weren't what I wanted them to be, my feelings that weren't what I wanted them to be, and my actions that weren't what I wanted them to be. And when any of those three were out of whack, I would be curious about them. I would ask myself questions about my reality, about my ways of seeing the world—my perceptions—that were getting in my way.

I was amazed at how quickly and effortlessly I was able to spark transforming realizations.

I'd think about what I was noticing, mostly in the spaces, as I bought groceries, or I waited for my sons to get out of school, or I was driving into town.

To my surprise, insights began to flow easily. My experimentation was unexpectedly productive, and I was amazed at how quickly and effortlessly

I was able to spark transforming realizations. Thrilled with the momentum, I wondered whether what I was doing would work for others.

I began to coach others to do what I had learned to do. I developed a method and called it xSAIL. A colleague, Fran Ritzenthaler, and I formed a company and began to certify experienced coaches in the xSAIL® Coaching methodology, providing them with a tool to deliver greater value to their clients and to distinguish themselves in their areas of expertise. It has been both exciting and gratifying to help individuals prime themselves for insight and then to watch as they are able quickly to generate life-altering epiphanies, often breaking through personal ceilings that have been in place for many years.

THE STUDY—AN OVERVIEW

As I noticed the impact of xSAIL Coaching in the lives of clients, I wondered what else I could learn about the mechanisms that create pivotal realizations. I was especially intrigued by stories of profound AHA!s that other people had, those intense moments of insight that seemed to arrive out of the blue. What could the experiences of others teach about having life-changing AHA!s?

> *I wondered what else I could learn about the mechanisms that create pivotal realizations.*

Sure, each momentous insight reveals its own important message. *Believe in yourself. Follow your passion. Spend time with the people you love.* But I had a hunch that there were even bigger lessons embedded in stories of life-altering AHA!s.

I decided to do a formal study to see if this hunch was correct.

My study would be a qualitative one, using data mining techniques. Then, if the study identified some common life lessons embedded in the stories, I would be able to build an empirically-based body of knowledge about transformational epiphanies.

I began by collecting a hundred published first-hand accounts of AHA!s. Then I studied them to see what there was to learn about such profound insights. The analysis confirmed my initial hunch. In fact, it was eye-opening. These stories of transformational AHA!s have a lot to teach. They carry evidence of unseen mechanisms that can, and do, create momentous realizations. Through that analysis, I was able to identify practical steps that an individual can take to spark life-changing epiphanies.

NELSON MANDELA—AN AHA! EXAMPLE

One significant example is the experience of Nelson Mandela. As a young man Nelson attended the University College of Fort Hare in Alice, South Africa. He studied hard, counted down the months to graduation, and pictured life after school. A college degree would take Nelson one step closer to his dreams. His life, however, would turn in ways he could not have imagined. Nelson experienced an epiphany so significant that he would later describe it in his autobiography *Long Walk to Freedom*.

Nelson experienced an epiphany so significant that he would later describe it in his autobiography Long Walk to Freedom.

Nelson's father had been a respected counselor to the rulers of Thembuland within the Xhosa nation. Nelson was still a boy when his father died, and the Thembu regent took the youngster into his care. The regent planned to groom young Nelson for the role his father had held. Proud to be a Thembu, Nelson prepared himself for that future.

Soon after turning sixteen, Nelson went away to boarding school, and after a few years he enrolled in college. As he was exposed to students and teachers from other tribes, his view of himself began to change. He saw that he wasn't only a Thembu or even an Xhosa. He was an African.

In his final year of college, Nelson returned home during a break. He had barely settled in when he received some shocking news. The regent of Thembuland had selected brides for his son, Justice, and his ward, Nelson. Dowries had been paid. The ceremonies were to take place right away.

Nelson and Justice realized that tribal custom gave the regent authority to orchestrate their marriages, but neither of them was ready. Instead the two young men defied the regent and ran away to Johannesburg.

In Johannesburg, Nelson worked as a law clerk, focused on finishing his degree, and made plans to go to law school. He struggled to live on a meager salary. To save money he skipped meals, walked six miles to work instead of riding the bus, and limited his work wardrobe to one well-patched suit. Eventually he moved to the Witwatersrand Native Labor Association (WNLA) compound where he could live rent-free.

The WNLA served as a recruiting agency for mineworkers, and the compound was a stopover for tribal leaders from across South Africa.

One day the queen regent of Basutoland and two of her chiefs visited the compound. Nelson chatted with the chiefs, enjoying their stories of his Thembu homeland. Then the queen addressed Nelson, but he didn't understand her. She had spoken in a tribal language, one Nelson didn't speak. The queen addressed Nelson again, this time asking in English, "What kind of lawyer and leader will you be who cannot speak the language of your people?"

The queen's comment triggered an insight for Nelson. He later recalled, "The question embarrassed and sobered me; it made me realize my parochialism and just how unprepared I was for the task of serving my people." After his AHA!, he made mid-course corrections while on his way to becoming South Africa's foremost leader.

Nelson Mandela's account is an example of the kinds of stories that I collected for the study—stories in which a flash of clarity had a significant, enduring impact on a person's life.

THE STUDY—THE DETAILS

The first phase of the study involved gathering published first-hand accounts of transformational epiphanies to supplement the ones that I had already begun to collect. I conducted data searches for terms and phrases such as "insight," "in that moment," and "I realized." I found accounts of momentous epiphanies in books, magazines, newspapers, and speeches. I found stories of profound AHA!s that detailed the experiences of people who are well known and those who aren't—Nelson Mandela, Tim Russert, Chandra Wilson, Dana Owens, and Pamela Klopfenstein, among many others.

Tim Russert experienced an epiphany as he held his newborn son for the first time. In that instant he understood the true depths of love and reordered his priorities, elevating fatherhood above career.

Chandra Wilson had a pivotal realization when she recognized that her mother loved her, even though that love was expressed in ways that Chandra would not have expected or chosen. Her AHA! let her release her worry and anger. It enabled her to allow her mother, and everyone in her life, to be who they would be.

Teenager Dana Owens had a flash of clarity when she received a standing ovation after her performance in the musical *The Wiz*. In that moment Dana recognized that she was fine just as she was, and she held onto that belief as she grew up to become the entertainer known as Queen Latifah.

Pamela Klopfenstein had an insight as she mourned the death of her four-year-old son, Jonathan. While reminiscing about the joys of caring for her son in the midst of his persistent medical issues, Pamela suddenly saw that she had lost her purpose after Jonathan died. In the days and weeks that followed, she set about creating a new sense of meaning in her life.

After locating each story, I would check to see if it was suitable for the study. In order to be included, the account needed to meet three criteria, regardless of whether the experience was labeled an insight, an epiphany, an aha, or a realization.

First of all, an account needed to include a flash of clarity. I looked for phrases such as "in that moment I saw," "then it hit me that," or "suddenly I knew."

Second, I looked for evidence that the person experiencing the AHA! gained a better understanding of the reality of a situation: Nelson Mandela saw that he wasn't prepared to lead. Tim Russert recognized that parenthood was more important to him than career. Chandra Wilson realized that love could be expressed in unexpected ways.

Third, each account needed to include evidence of a significant and enduring impact on the person who experienced the insight. For example, Nelson Mandela changed what he was doing to prepare himself to be a leader, Tim Russert made being a father a priority, and Chandra Wilson embraced different approaches to living life.

As I set out to collect accounts of life-changing insights, I considered the sample size that I would need. Theoretical sampling (rather than statistical sampling) would be appropriate given that the research was aimed at building a theory rather than evaluating one. With theoretical sampling, the goal was to include a sufficient number of published accounts so that by the time I was finishing the analysis I wouldn't be learning anything new about the characteristics of transformational insights (what researchers call "theoretical saturation"). At the outset, I didn't know how many accounts I would need to reach theoretical saturation for the group being studied—twenty-five, fifty, or more. Eventually, I decided to include an initial sample of one hundred stories, expecting that number would probably be plenty. If it weren't I had the option with theoretical sampling to gather additional accounts. (I finished the analysis with ninety-nine, having eliminated one, and as it turned out, the sample size was adequate to reach theoretical saturation.)

I considered the sample size that I would need.

In the second phase of the study, I used what's called a constant comparative method to simultaneously code and analyze the data. To do that I read through printed copies of the accounts one at a time. I looked for as many characteristics of insights as possible. As I noted each characteristic in an account, I would compare it to what I had already seen—initially account-to-account and later, as the patterns in the data became clearer and better developed, account-to-characteristic. Once

I decided to include an initial sample of one hundred stories.

all the accounts had been coded, I was able to compare the characteristics with an eye to clarity, logic, simplicity, and relevance. As a result I retained most categories, combined some categories, and eliminated others.

THE BOOK

This book is the result of my research. *The AHA! Handbook: How to spark the insights that will transform your life and career* describes twenty-one epiphany-encouraging actions. You can take these twenty-one actions to transform your life. The actions fall into three phases.

Phase One: Prime Yourself. You can live life in a way that attracts pivotal realizations. This section shows you how: Go ahead, live *your* life. Be alert in the good times and in the bad. Think, but don't overdo it. Focus on your feelings. Wonder about your current situation. Notice what's real for you. (It might not be what you think.) And, be willing to let go.

Phase Two: Watch for Triggers. Certain events tend to trigger profound epiphanies. You can capitalize on such moments to ignite your own pivotal realizations. The four triggers in this section point the way.

Trigger 1—Catch a glimpse of yourself. See yourself clearly. And see yourself through the eyes of others.

Trigger 2—Catch a glimpse of others. See others clearly. And understand their perspective.

Trigger 3—Follow the lead of your VIPs (Very Important People). Hear what they are saying. Notice what they are doing. Beware, though, of what's not a fit for you.

Trigger 4—Discover a new perspective in distressful situations. Be observant during life's harrowing moments. However, don't trouble trouble by taking unneeded risks.

Phase Three: Capture the Value. Once you've had a pivotal AHA!, you can take additional actions to boost its impact in your life. This section explains how: Clarify the message. Try it on to make sure it fits. Get to work. And, go for gold!

The description of each epiphany-encouraging action begins with a representative story, flows to a summary of the data, and includes additional brief examples that demonstrate the richness of the findings. It then returns to the representative story to highlight the transformational effect of the insight. Each description concludes with "A Note to You," practical advice you can use to spark your own pivotal AHA!.

▼ ▼ ▼

As for Nelson Mandela, two years after his transformational insight, he joined the African National Congress (ANC). The year was 1944. Soon members of the ANC began to resist the apartheid policies of the South African government.

In 1963 Nelson Mandela and other ANC members were arrested on charges of sabotage. They were tried and sentenced to life in prison.

In 1990, after spending almost thirty years behind bars, Nelson Mandela was released. The next year he was elected president of the ANC. In 1994 black South Africans were allowed to vote for the first time, and Nelson Mandela was elected the President of South Africa.

Nelson Mandela began to step away from public life in 2004. In his book *Conversations with Myself,* he said that he was looking forward to having time to read whatever he chose—including African literature written in a variety of tribal languages, not only in his native tongue.

▼ ▼ ▼

Unfortunately, life-altering AHA!s, such as the one that Nelson Mandela experienced, are as rare as they are powerful. We accept that they happen in their own time, if ever. We understand that they operate outside a person's control—the product of fate, luck, or chance. So says our collective wisdom.

But what if our collective wisdom is wrong? What if the impossible *is* possible? Can each of us take proactive steps to spark pivotal epiphanies in our lives? I'm confident that we can. I've seen it happen—first with myself and then with others.

The seemingly impossible *is* possible. Stories of AHA!s point the way.

A NOTE TO YOU

Would you like to tap the power of insight to transform your life? You can! There are three phases:

Prime yourself for a flash of clarity.

Watch for the triggers that can spark an AHA!.

Take steps to capture the full value of your epiphany.

What are you waiting for?

Prime Yourself

▼ ▼ ▼

This section is not about priming yourself to have an ordinary, run-of-the-mill creative aha. Instead, it will show you how to prepare yourself to have the kind of AHA! that will rock your world—a profound epiphany, a life-changing insight, a pivotal realization.

▼ ▼ ▼

Go ahead, live *your* life

Ten-year-old Chitra Banerjee Divakaruni was miserable. It was a summer day in her hometown of Calcutta, and she was stuck indoors. Outside the monsoon sky hung dark with clouds. Warm, heavy rain whipped about in the wind. Floodwater poured through the streets. It was a day that would change Chitra's life—a day she would later describe in *O, The Oprah Magazine.*

It wasn't the weather that trapped Chitra inside. At that very moment her brother and possibly every other child in the neighborhood were playing outside. They were enjoying the spectacular day—running about, racing their homemade paper boats, getting drenched. Chitra didn't need to see them to know what they were doing, because she had always been there with them. Today was different.

Today Chitra's mother informed her that her paper-boat-floating days were over. Done. For a ten-year-old it was no longer proper. Chitra protested. Her older brother was allowed to play in the rain. Why couldn't she? Her mother stood firm.

What had happened to the mother who had been her supporter and champion?

"You're a girl," she said. Chitra listened in disbelief. What had happened to the mother who had been her supporter and champion?

Chitra moped about the house searching for something to do. She spied her brother's Indian history textbook lying on a desk and took a peek inside. As she leafed through the pages, she found little more than endless paragraphs punctuated by an occasional picture. Then an illustration caught Chitra's eye and lured her into the text.

In the picture a woman sat on a tiger skin wearing medieval men's clothing and reaching for a sword. The woman was Sultana Raziyya who had ruled over Delhi in the thirteenth century. No woman had done so before, and no woman would do so again until Chitra's lifetime.

Raziyya hadn't automatically risen to the throne after the death of her father, the Sultan. Her father had recognized her keen political skills and had chosen her to succeed him. But the noblemen in Delhi resisted being led by a woman.

Raziyya stood against the opposition, eventually taking command. She ruled wisely—creating order, building infrastructure, and addressing discrimination. Some of the noblemen disagreed with her liberal policies and revolted. Sultana Raziyya fought to keep the throne, and died in battle.

As Chitra read about the Sultana, she experienced an epiphany. She saw that she too could resist expectations that limited who she was and whom she could become. "I promised myself that, like Raziyya, I wouldn't give up," Chitra recounted in the magazine.

▼ ▼ ▼

The accounts of transformational insights included in this study are touching, uplifting, and inspirational. But are they likely to spark life-changing realizations in readers just as learning about the Sultana ignited an AHA! for Chitra? The study shows that the answer is no. Reading about the experiences of others triggered momentous insights in only three percent of the cases.

Pivotal epiphanies don't occur while people are contemplating the lives of others in a third-person, abstract way. They arise when people are immersed in living their lives.

Profound AHA!s can emerge amid the extraordinary events of life.

Trudie Styler had a life-changing epiphany as she swam against the current of a Brazilian river and almost drowned. In a burst of clarity, she saw that she had allowed other people to direct her destiny, and she vowed to take control of her life.

Andre Agassi had a pivotal realization after he became the number-one ranked tennis player in the world. In a jolt of understanding, he discovered his greatest career aspiration—a goal he had quashed because it seemed unreachable.

Alan Alda had an epiphany as he lay in a hospital bed in Chile awaiting emergency surgery. In a flash of insight, he gained a new perspective on death—and life.

Momentous insights can also emerge during the routine events of life.

Tracy Chevalier had a life-changing realization one morning at work as she listened to criticism from her boss. In that instant Tracy knew it was time to return to school for a master's degree where she could focus on her writing.

Chef Curtis Stone had an AHA! as he stood at his stove trying to create a perfect omelet. In a flash of clarity, he understood that taste trumped technique and set out on a mission to simplify his approach to cooking, and to help others do the same.

Janice Schnake Greene had an epiphany as she stood cheering from the sideline at her daughter's soccer game. In that moment she saw that childhood regrets were keeping her from being the mother she wanted to be.

Transformational realizations arrive in the midst of living life, occurring during exceptional events as well as in day-to-day routines. That held true even for the three individuals in the study whose insights were triggered when reading about the experiences of others—Chitra, Jenna Fischer, and Gail Buckley.

Chitra was struggling to come to terms with her mother's changing expectations when she discovered Sultana Raziyya. Learning about the Sultana sparked an epiphany for Chitra that gave her the freedom to forge her own path.

Teenaged Jenna Fischer was brooding in her bedroom when she found a journal from the year she was born. As she read what her parents had written and saw their love for her, she experienced an insight. It gave her an abiding gratitude for her mother and father—and has helped her to anchor her interactions with them in love.

Gail Buckley was decluttering her house when she stumbled on a rich family history in a musty trunk. As she explored the lives of her ancestors, she experienced an AHA!. It revealed to her the long, unrecognized presence of a black middle class in the United States, and led her to capture her family's story in her book *The Hornes: An American family*.

Pivotal epiphanies arose in the study when people were actively engaged in their lives, whether they were deep in their daily routines or in the midst of unique experiences.

▼ ▼ ▼

As for ten-year-old Chitra, she remained true to the promise she made herself, refusing to allow the expectations of others to limit who she could become. In 1976 she immigrated to the United States. She worked odd jobs to pay for her education and eventually earned a Ph.D. from the University of California at Berkeley.

Chitra has become a well-regarded author and poet. Her work has been published in more than fifty magazines and translated into twenty languages. She has written a number of books, two of which have been made into movies.

The stories that Chitra has brought to life in many ways reflect her experience on that long-ago, rainy day in Calcutta. "The women in these stories are in transition, caught in the border between a traditional patriarchal society and a world of possibilities and choice," wrote reviewer Rocio Davis in an analysis of Chitra's work.

▼ ▼ ▼

Life happens. And it's in the day-to-day experience of living it where pivotal insights reside.

A NOTE TO YOU

Take a quick scan of your life. Are there areas that you're avoiding while you hope for inspiration to strike?

Don't put your life on hold. Immerse yourself in it.

Recognize that AHA!s reside in your life—not separately from it.

*Go ahead. Live **your** life.*

Be alert in the good times and in the bad

In the mid 1970s Bill Rees was a young professor at the University of British Columbia. He knew what he wanted and was determined to achieve it. He wanted to calculate the effect that humans have on the environment, but he struggled to find a suitable measure.

Years passed. One night Bill awoke to a flash of insight. He saw that to solve his dilemma he simply needed to invert the formula he had been using. Over time he fine-tuned the new calculation, eventually calling the output the "ecological footprint" of humans.

Bill's method to measure mankind's impact has been widely adopted. It's used by the United Nations, by the World Wildlife Fund, and by other organizations and individuals around the globe.

Bill had dedicated himself to the study of human ecology decades before he became a professor. He was still a boy when he discovered his life's mission. It also came to him in an insight. He would later recount the day in interviews with Deborah Jones for *Times Canada* and with Mike

> *He was still a boy when he discovered his life's mission.*

Gismondi for *Aurora Online.*

Bill grew up in the Canadian Province of Ontario, where farming was a family affair. He and his eight cousins helped their grandparents work the land. It was a time before wires brought electricity to rural places and before farmers bought tractors to tend their fields.

One July day was delightfully warm and sunny. Bill and his cousins had been hard at work in the field all morning. When they heard the call to lunch, they didn't hesitate.

The children gathered with the adults on the wide porch of the farmhouse. The table was piled high with roast beef, chicken, carrots, baby potatoes, lettuce, apple pie, and more. Bill sat down and began to eat. As he looked at the food on his plate, he was struck by an epiphany that arrived with a shiver. He recognized that he had helped raise each and every item he was about to consume. "I had an overwhelming sense of being connected to the earth—that we are, literally, what we eat," he told Jones.

▼ ▼ ▼

Necessity is the mother of invention. That adage proved true for Bill at work. He had a driving need to measure the impact of humans on their environment. It was *his* necessity. Then in an insight, he discovered the concept of an ecological footprint.

Is necessity also the mother of life-changing AHA!s? It can be, but is not a requirement. In the study, momentous epiphanies occurred along the full range of experiences—from the desperate (13%) through to the uncomfortable (73%) and on to the divine (12%).

Transformational realizations can strike during times of contentment, times of ease, and times of pleasure. That was the case in twelve percent of the accounts in the study, including those of

Bill, Rocco DiSpirito, and Gene Wilder.

Six-year-old Rocco DiSpirito had an insight when he witnessed the allure of his mother's cooking. He had watched his mother as she worked in her tiny kitchen. Soon the air was filled with the aroma of a frittata, a baked Italian omelet. As Rocco reached for a slice fresh from the oven, his mother told him he would have to wait. The frittata was for the women of the Rosary Society.

Is necessity also the mother of life-changing AHA!s?

Rocco's mother covered the pan, and the two of them walked to church. The women of the Rosary Society were thrilled with the frittata. As Rocco saw their delight and thankfulness, he experienced a powerful realization. It showed him how sharing a meal could create a sense of community, and led him to become a chef.

Gene Wilder was eleven years old when an awe-inspiring event triggered an insight for him. Seated in a small auditorium, he waited for a performance to begin. The hall was packed with people, and everyone seemed to talk at once.

The house lights dimmed. The room grew quiet. A spotlight illuminated the stage. In it stood Gene's teenage sister. As she recited *The Necklace* by Guy de Maupassant, the audience was spellbound. Gene noticed the reaction and was struck by a pivotal AHA!. It showed him the power of a performer and prompted him to become an entertainer.

Momentous epiphanies also emerge during times of discomfort, times of uncertainty, and times of unease. That was the case in a large majority (73%) of the accounts in the study, such as those of Josh Groban and Nora Ephron.

Josh Groban was a freshman in high school when an uncomfortable situation sparked a key insight for him.

Josh had felt out of place in middle school. He had few friends, he wasn't into sports, and he wasn't into studying. Instead he preferred to sit alone at home composing songs and making music.

Fall arrived. Josh had applied and been accepted to the Los Angeles County High School for the Arts. On the first day of class, a teacher asked Josh to perform an impromptu monologue. He did, but thought he had bombed.

Josh worried that his new school would be no better than the previous one. Then fellow classmates gushed about his performance. Josh looked around and noticed other students engrossed in one art form or another. As he caught a clear view of his peers, he experienced a powerful AHA!. It highlighted for him the rewards of focusing on his passion, and gave him the resolve to always do so.

Josh worried that his new school would be no better than the previous one

Nora Ephron was waiting in frustration for a movie to begin when a friend's comment triggered a pivotal realization for her. She had sat in the small screening room and watched as the space became crowded and then overflowed. People stood helplessly in the aisles. In her take-control, solve-the-problem way, Nora saw an easy fix. And, she was irritated and baffled that no one else seemed to know what to do. Just bring in extra chairs!

Nora shared her solution with the friend sitting next to her, and later recounted his reply in her book *I Feel Bad About My Neck*.

"Nora, we can't do everything," the friend responded. In a flash of clarity, Nora got the message. She was able to relax and let others figure things out for themselves—there in the screening room *and* in the other areas of her life.

Transformational insights can also occur in desperate situations, such as a near-death experience, the loss of a loved one, or a threat to one's family or career. That was the case in thirteen percent of the accounts in the study, including those of Cynthia Nixon and Iman.

Cynthia Nixon experienced a life-altering epiphany when she faced losing custody of her children. She had grown up watching her parents argue. When they separated she went to live with her mother, Anne.

Anne was finished with fighting, so she and Cynthia forged a pact. They wouldn't debate. They wouldn't argue. The person who felt most strongly about an issue would win, while the other one would surrender.

Press or concede. Cynthia carried that approach with her into adulthood, but it didn't work well with her partner, Danny Mozes. Eventually they separated.

Cynthia and Danny both wanted custody of their children, and neither was willing to yield. The situation sparked a pivotal AHA! for Cynthia. Her new perspective opened the possibility of seeking a middle ground with Danny, and gave her the courage to speak her mind in all areas of her life.

Iman had been in a serious automobile accident when she had a life-changing realization. It was a Friday evening, and Iman had just finished dinner with friends. The supermodel caught a taxi and headed home. Her cab had just entered an intersection when a drunk driver ran a red light. The car collided with the taxi. The taxi crashed into a building, and Iman slammed into the glass partition that separated her from the driver.

Iman lay in a hospital bed in agony. She had broken a number of bones in her face and torso. The doctor showed her some pre-crash photos and assured her that she would heal with little scarring. As Iman looked at the pictures of herself, she was struck by the recognition that she didn't want to be the person she had been.

She was struck by the recognition that she didn't want to be the person she had been.

In the days and weeks that followed, she focused on recovering her health, and on cultivating an inner beauty she had lacked before the accident.

Necessity is the mother of invention. The adage held true in some, but not all, of the accounts in the study. Transformational insights occurred along a lengthy continuum of experiences—from the desperate through to the uneasy and on to the delightful.

▼ ▼ ▼

As for young Bill Rees, he was so moved on that warm July day by his sense of kinship with the Earth that he couldn't finish his lunch.

Years later Bill went to college planning to major in human ecology. He was flabbergasted to find that he had chosen a course of study that didn't exist. At that time the field of ecology focused exclusively on nonhuman species. So Bill majored in zoology and biology, while keeping a constant search for researchers and practitioners whose work aligned with his insight-inspired passion.

After graduating, Bill struggled to find a job that fit his career interest. He was thrilled when a former mentor created a joint position in resource ecology and planning at the University of British Columbia. Bill applied and was hired.

▼ ▼ ▼

AHAs! arise along the full range of human experiences from the desperate to the divine.

A NOTE TO YOU

How's your life at the moment?

Is it frightening, distressing, or heart-breaking? Is it unsettled, trying, or difficult? Is it satisfying, enjoyable, and rewarding?

Be watchful wherever you are. Your epiphany is waiting for you there.

Be alert in the good times and in the bad.

Think, but don't overdo it

The 1993 tennis season was a difficult one for Andre Agassi. Tendonitis in his wrist limited his playing time, and impacted his performance. He returned to Wimbledon as the defending champion—and lost in the quarterfinals. He read in *USA Today* that his coach had quit, before a FedEx package arrived with the news.

Andre began the 1994 season with a surgically repaired wrist, a new coach, and high hopes. After a string of disappointing losses, things began to turn. Late in the season Andre competed in the U.S. Open and won. He traveled to the Australian Open early in 1995. There he defeated Pete Sampras in three straight sets.

Pete was ranked the number one tennis player in the world. Andre's coach, his trainer, and his manager all decided it was time to unseat Pete. Andre agreed. Their decision would spark a chain of events that would lead Andre to a pivotal insight, one that he would describe in his autobiography, *Open*.

Focused on overtaking Pete, Andre spent his days at the gym training with renewed passion. Meanwhile, his trainer undertook a worldwide search for the best thinking in fitness and nutrition. Their efforts paid off as Andre reached peak condition.

Andre faced off against Pete at Indian Wells but lost. At Key Biscayne he met Pete again. Andre lost the first set, won the second, and battled to a tie in the third. The outcome hinged on a tiebreaker, and Andre prevailed, winning seven to three.

Andre caught a plane to Palermo, Italy, where he would play in the Davis Cup. He made his way to his hotel and checked in. The phone rang. It was his manager calling to say that the latest computer rankings had just been released. Andre had done it! He was the number one tennis player in the world.

Soon a reporter called. Andre told the reporter that he was pleased with the ranking. He lied. In fact, he felt nothing.

Andre wandered the streets of Palermo. He downed cups of strong black coffee and thought about his career. He considered retiring but knew that wouldn't solve his problem. What he needed was a new goal, a goal that meant something to him. But what? Eventually Andre decided he wanted one thing. He wanted to win all four tennis Grand Slams. He had one to go—the French Open.

Andre felt a surge of energy as he thought about this new goal. He noticed his excitement and had an epiphany, calling it a sudden and shocking insight. He realized that he had always wanted to take all four Grand Slams. He wrote that he had "simply repressed the desire because it didn't seem possible."

▼ ▼ ▼

Logical thinking is a valuable tool. It can produce sound decisions, solve vexing problems, and overcome daunting challenges. In Andre's case, logical thinking helped him to clarify his career goal.

Logical thinking can also lay the foundation for a pivotal AHA!. As Andre observed the energy he felt for his new goal, he had an insight that reinforced his desire to win all four Grand Slams.

Andre was not alone. Analysis seemed to set the stage for epiphanies in twenty-six percent of the accounts in the study, including those of Hillary Rodham Clinton, Timothy Hutton, and Suzan-Lori Parks.

In 1999 Hillary Rodham Clinton experienced a pivotal AHA! as she contemplated a run for the United States Senate. Hillary had consulted others, weighed the situation, and examined the hurdles. Still she vacillated, unable to decide.

In the midst of her uncertainty, Hillary accepted an invitation to speak at an event focused on wom-

Logical thinking can also lay the foundation for a pivotal AHA!

en's participation in sports. The day of the speech arrived, and she joined Billy Jean King and Dominique Dawes at the Lab School in Manhattan's Chelsea neighborhood.

The captain of the girl's basketball team at the school, Sofia Totti, introduced Hillary to the audience. Sofia later recalled the day in an interview with Maura Yates for *The New York Sun*. The teenager had shaken Hillary's hand and whispered a message to the First Lady, "Dare to compete, Mrs. Clinton. Dare to compete."

The girl's words sparked a powerful epiphany for Hillary. She saw for the first time that her hesitance to run for office was out of sync with the advice she had given other women. That realization gave her the nudge she needed to enter the race.

Nineteen-year-old Timothy Hutton experienced a life-changing insight as he sat lost in thought on the New York City subway. He idly thumbed through his new passport, picturing the places it could take him. But then he remembered all the things he needed to do. He had phone calls to make. He had a script to review. He had to decide whether he even wanted a career in acting. On top of it all, Timothy needed to come to terms with his father's recent death. He had been so busy filming *Ordinary People* that he hadn't even had enough time to do that.

In the midst of his musing, Timothy was struck by an AHA!. He saw that despite all that he had to do, he didn't need to be any particular place. He was free to be anywhere! Timothy quickly homed in on a new destination—the airport. There he bought a ticket to Paris. His new philosophy gave him three days to explore the city and map his future. And, it gave him an ongoing readiness to seize the moment.

Suzan-Lori Parks arrived at an epiphany after analyzing a predicament from every angle. She had landed a position as playwright in residence at a theater. The theater, however, refused to produce any of her plays. Heartbroken and angry, Suzan-Lori considered her options but couldn't find a viable alternative. She needed the money, so she stopped writing, reported to work every day, and pitched in to help.

Days and weeks passed until one day an insight changed the way Suzan-Lori viewed the situation. She suddenly recognized that no one could prevent her from being who she was—a playwright. She began to write again and within three days had created a play that would earn her a Pulitzer Prize.

Logical thinking can set the stage for a profound insight. It can frame the problem, expose the obstacles, and enumerate the options. However, logical thinking probably won't lead straight to a life-changing realization. That's because epiphanies don't flow directly from analysis. Instead they break the line of reasoning, occurring as a spontaneous thought. They bring a new way of seeing things and are often accompanied by a distinct physical sensation—a flash, a shock, a shiver.

Epiphanies don't flow directly from analysis.

▼ ▼ ▼

As for Andre, he achieved his goal in 1999 when he won his fourth Grand Slam—the French Open. At the time he was twenty-nine years old, well past his prime by the standards of professional tennis. He went on to win four more Grand Slam titles—the U.S. Open that same year and the Australian Open in 2000, 2001, and 2003. By doing so he became the only professional tennis player to win more Grand Slam titles after turning twenty-nine than he did before that age.

▼ ▼ ▼

Thinking analytically can lay the foundation for a life-changing realization, but it's not likely to deliver one directly.

A NOTE TO YOU

Think through your situation. What does your analysis tell you?

Logical thinking can help you size up a challenge, consider your alternatives, and home in on a solution.

Logical thinking can also set the stage for a pivotal insight, but it's not likely to lead you directly to one.

So, think, but don't overdo it.

Focus on your feelings

Marcia Gay Harden inched her car through a Washington, D.C., traffic jam. The twenty-three-year-old must have been quite a sight. She sat in her yellow VW Beetle convertible in a Snow White costume crying. The traffic hadn't caused Marcia's tears—although it certainly hadn't helped. Marcia's problem was that she needed to be in two places at once.

She needed to be in a performance that morning, a production of the Make-A-Wish Foundation. The stage was a patient's room at Georgetown University Hospital. The audience was Bonnie, a seven-year-old with cancer. Bonnie had made her wish. She wanted to meet Snow White.

She sat in her yellow VW Beetle convertible in a Snow White costume crying.

Marcia also needed to be at a casting call. Oliver Stone was in town. *The* Oliver Stone who had won an Academy Award for his screenplay *Midnight Express*. He was selecting crowd-scene extras for the movie *Born on the Fourth of July*. Marcia was convinced this was going to be her big break. She just knew it.

In a panic, Marcia had tried to reschedule her appearance as Snow White. It wasn't an option. Bonnie didn't have much time left. Marcia also had tried to reschedule the casting call. That wasn't an option, either. Oliver Stone was in town for just one day.

Bonnie or Oliver Stone? Marcia had to choose. The choice she made that day would result in an insight. She would write about it in a *Guideposts* article and talk about it in a commencement speech at the University of Texas.

Late into the night Marcia had wrestled with her choices. Eventually she decided to contact the Make-A-Wish Foundation to cancel. Morning came. Marcia couldn't bring herself to make the call. Instead, she phoned the casting agency.

> *"I realized that what I had wanted was not what I had needed."*

Marcia arrived at the hospital and raced inside. She made one last desperate call to the casting director. She was told that the audition would go on without her.

Outside Bonnie's room, Marcia paused. She inhaled deeply, composed herself, and stepped through the doorway.

Snow White found Bonnie seated on a cot. The small, frail girl brightened when she saw her visitor. Snow White told Bonnie that she wished that the dwarfs had been able to come, and she talked about Prince Charming.

Bonnie interrupted. She wanted to know what would happen when she died. Would Prince Charming be there to kiss her and wake her up?

Marcia was dumbfounded. What could she say? She paused, and somehow the right words came. She told Bonnie that something better would happen. The kiss that would wake her would come from God.

Bonnie's question ignited an epiphany for Marcia. "In that seminal moment, I realized that what I had wanted was not what I had needed," she told the University of Texas audience. Marcia had wanted fame. What she needed was a purpose beyond herself.

▼ ▼ ▼

In the study, transformational insights linked closely to emotions. They occurred in the midst of life's joys and sorrows, hopes and fears, excitement and uncertainties. Karen Watson, for example, was feeling blue when an AHA! struck, while Emily Procter was feeling isolated. Kyra Sedgwick was dispirited, Dana Delany was panicked, and Eckhart Tolle was desperate.

It had been twenty years since Karen Watson graduated from high school. During that time she had worked hard to build a successful career, but she wasn't happy.

At her class reunion Karen had an epiphany, and in that moment she saw that she was living a one-dimensional existence dominated by her work. In the days that followed, Karen focused on creating better balance in her life—and soon had set her sights on preparing for an Ironman triathlon.

Emily Procter was feeling isolated when she experienced a pivotal realization. She had graduated from college and moved to Los Angeles. She had lived in the city for four years and was making progress building her acting career, but she still felt unconnected and alone.

One autumn day, Emily was struck with an AHA!, and in an instant she saw the source

She saw that she was living a one-dimensional existence dominated by her work.

of her problem. Except for her cat, all she thought about was herself—how she looked, whether she was making progress in her career. Emily immediately changed her focus and began to volunteer in her community where she found friendship, inspiration, and contentment.

Kyra Sedgwick was feeling disturbed by the state of the planet when she was hit by a powerful AHA!. Ever the urban dweller, Kyra had never given much thought to her surroundings. Things changed, though, when she became pregnant. She began to focus on creating a safe and healthy environment for her son—initially in her womb and later in their home.

As baby Travis grew, Kyra saw that she wouldn't be able to protect him from every danger. Then in a jolt of understanding, she recognized that the well-being of her son was tied to the health of the Earth, and she began to advocate for the environment.

Dana Delany had worked herself into a complete state of panic when she experienced a life-changing epiphany. She and her friends had gone to a spa in honor of her fortieth birthday. Finished with a salt scrub, Dana climbed into a steam cabinet. With only her head exposed, she watched as the spa attendant secured the cabinet door, started the treatment, and left the room.

One minute passed, then two. The walls of the cabinet seemed to slide in close around Dana. She tried everything to calm herself, but nothing worked. Determined not to call for help, she desperately felt around inside the box. Where's the latch? No latch, only panic.

After the eternity of a few minutes, the attendant returned. Dana announced that she was finished. She tried to appear calm, but was unable to hide the creak in her voice.

The attendant reached over and casually pulled the door open. There was no latch! Dana could have opened the door at any time. In a flash of clarity Dana got the message and laughed, realizing that the steam cabinet was a metaphor for her life. That realization stayed with her in the months and years that followed, calming and guiding her.

Eckhart Tolle was feeling desperate when he was struck by an AHA!—one that he would write about in his book *The Power of Now.* Eckhart had awakened in the middle of the night to a familiar sense of dread. That night the feeling was so strong that it overpowered his desire to live.

"I cannot live with myself any longer," he said to himself again, and again. In a flash of clarity, Eckhart recognized two distinct aspects of that thought. It was if there were two Eckharts— "myself"(the source of his negative feelings) and "I" (the one who found "myself" unbearable and was finished with the relationship). Perhaps one of those personalities was an illusion, Eckhart speculated. The epiphany sparked a profoundly spiritual experience for him and set him on the mission of sharing his newfound understanding with others.

In many cases in the study, individuals reported experiencing emotions prior to life-changing insights. In eighty-four percent of the cases, those emotions were explicitly described. What about the other sixteen percent? Did the epiphanics in those accounts arise in the midst of cool, emotionless lives? The answer is a clear no. In each of those incidents, it's reasonable to infer that emotions were present prior to the insight but not described in the account. The stories of Evonne Goolagong and Jay Leno were included in this group.

> *Eckhart Tolle was feeling desperate when he was struck by an AHA!*

Evonne Goolagong had an insight when her mother died. She later recalled the experience in an interview with Jeff Pearlman for *Sports Illustrated.* Although the emotions Evonne felt prior to her insight were not specified in the account, they were implied.

Evonne had not lived in her homeland of Australia since she was thirteen years old. When she was thirty-nine she traveled home to attend her mother's funeral. As Evonne observed the traditions of her Aborigine people, she was struck by an epiphany. In that moment she saw that she needed to return to her beginnings in order to discover who she was. Soon Evonne and her family had relocated to Noosa in the Australian state of Queensland, and then she embarked on an emotional path of self-discovery.

She needed to return to her beginnings in order to discover who she was.

Eight-year-old Jay Leno had an AHA! when another boy brought a risqué photo to the playground. Decades later he described the experience in *O, The Oprah Magazine.* Even though Jay didn't specify the emotions he experienced before the insight, he hinted at them.

Young Jay didn't like to play with children his own age. He preferred to hang around a group of eleven- and twelve-year-old boys. The older children weren't known to be model citizens. They would pilfer chewing gum from stores and monkey around with pocketknives.

When one of the boys bragged that he had pornography, everyone drew close, angling for a peek. In that moment Jay caught a clear view of where those boys were headed. He didn't lean in with the others to take a look. Instead, he walked away. And in the decades that followed, he kept his eye on the long view.

Pivotal epiphanies in this study occurred in the midst of emotional experiences, whether the feelings were explicitly described in the accounts or implied.

▼ ▼ ▼

As for Marcia Gay Harden, she eventually earned her Screen Actors Guild union card and relocated to New York City. There she continued to struggle and to aspire. She finally got the break she was looking for a few years later when she landed a role in *Miller's Crossing*, a movie by young filmmakers Joel and Ethan Coen. Since then Marcia has performed in many roles on stage, in film, and on television. In 2000 she received an Academy Award for Best Supporting Actress for her performance in *Pollock*.

The epiphany sparked by Bonnie's question has stayed with Marcia. It has given her a purpose in her work—one that has guided her to meaningful roles and bestowed the joy of knowing that she has impacted lives.

▼ ▼ ▼

Transformational AHA!s don't strike when people are living lives of cool detachment. They emerge when people are engaged emotionally in the events of their lives.

A NOTE TO YOU

Where's the feeling, the emotion, and the passion in your life?

Don't strive to live a calm, unemotional existence. You won't find your insight there.

You'll find it in the joys, in the sorrows, in the excitement, in the struggles, and in the surprises that await you.

As you go about your days, focus on your feelings.

Wonder about
your current situation

Dayna Smith led a very busy life in Buford, Georgia. She took care of her family, managed the household, and ran a preschool for two hundred children. One evening she made an important discovery. She found she was neglecting a critical aspect of life and would later describe her realization in *Guideposts* magazine.

It was almost dinnertime. Dayna stood at the stove frying ground beef in a cast iron skillet. As she tried to lift the pan from the burner, she found she didn't have the strength to move it and had to call to her teenage daughter for help.

Dayna focused on finishing dinner while she thought about what had just happened. What was wrong? Why couldn't she lift the pan? At first she explained away the episode, but then she caught herself. She knew that her lack of strength was tied to a bigger issue—one that had started with a broken foot.

Dayna had fractured her foot twice. The first time she tripped over a step while taking care of her grandmother. The doctor put Dayna's foot in a cast and told her not to walk on it, but she didn't follow the doctor's orders. Her family needed her.

Dayna's foot healed slowly—so slowly that the doctor recommended a bone density test. Again, Dayna didn't follow the medical advice. She was too busy starting a preschool.

The second time Dayna broke her foot, she hit it against the bed frame while making her son's bed. This time the bone healed even more slowly, and she went for a bone density scan.

Dayna's bone density was below normal. The doctor prescribed medication, supplements, exercise, and dietary changes. He warned Dayna that her condition, if untreated, could lead to osteoporosis. She started the medication, but stopped after a month. Two years had passed while she didn't follow the doctor's orders.

Dayna leaned back against the kitchen counter and worried. Had her denial caught up with her? Wasn't she too young to have bone disease? Was it too late to do something?

"How on earth could I have been so good at doling out advice all these years—and so deaf to my own problems?"

That night Dayna lay awake in bed. She was afraid. She prayed, asking what she should do. She also thought about those in her family who had suffered from osteoporosis. Her mind wandered back to a former job where she had assessed children for developmental disabilities. One case in particular came to mind. The mother couldn't believe that her kindergarten daughter needed special help. Dayna had done her best to reassure the mom as they reviewed treatment options for the girl.

As Dayna thought about that mother, she experienced an insight. She recognized in herself the same kind of denial. "How on earth could I have been so good at doling out advice all these years—and so deaf to my own problems?" Dana asked herself.

▼ ▼ ▼

Dayna had asked herself a number of questions prior to her insight. Was she paying for her denial? Was it too late to make a difference? What could she do? She didn't find immediate answers to her questions. Instead, curiosity about her situation appeared to have set the stage for a life-changing insight.

Asking questions seemed to lay the groundwork for pivotal realizations in thirty-five percent of the cases in the study. The percentage was even higher in situations where a person felt uneasy before an epiphany. In those cases, fifty percent of the individuals reported posing questions prior to a profound AHA!. That group included, among others, Bernie Mac, Carmindy Bowyer, and Halle Berry.

As Bernie Mac questioned his choice of careers, he had a crucial insight that he would later describe in an interview with Scott Frampton for *O, The Oprah Magazine*.

Bernie was in his early twenties and had a problem. He loved being a comedian but earned next to nothing doing it. So he pieced together work as he struggled to provide for his family. In one job Bernie sold beer at Chicago Bears football games. During one game, Bernie took a serious fall while he was working the stands. He was lucky to have survived. Rattled, he went home early.

As Bernie sat in his apartment fretting over his finances and questioning his focus on comedy, he thought about his deceased mother. "Always give your best," she used to say. Her words played through his mind and sparked an epiphany. In that moment Bernie renewed his commitment to his craft, recognizing that he and his audiences deserved nothing less than his greatest effort.

Carmindy Bowyer was wondering whether she could make a positive impact on others when she had a powerful epiphany.

At eighteen, she had landed a job working at a cosmetics

counter. Women would come in for makeovers, and Carmindy would demonstrate the products. Many of the women would point out their flaws, but Carmindy would highlight each customer's unique beauty.

Carmindy had been hired to sell makeup, but that wasn't her goal. Her passion was to help women feel better about themselves. She wondered, though, what she could do in the limited time she had with each person. Then the heartfelt gratitude of one customer sparked a pivotal AHA! for Carmindy. It showed her the impact she could make and reinforced her choice of careers.

As Halle Berry asked herself the same question over and over again, she arrived at a life-changing insight. It was one so significant that she would later describe it in an article for *O, The Oprah Magazine*.

Halle sat at her kitchen table. She was bleeding but didn't know why. The last thing she remembered was driving through an intersection near her home.

Although Halle had no memory of it, she had been involved in an accident. The District Attorney considered the incident a hit and run and took weeks deciding whether to charge Halle with a felony. Halle spent that time feeling sick with anxiety. "Why is this happening?" she asked herself again and again.

The D.A. eventually charged Halle with a misdemeanor. As part of her sentence, she was required to perform community service. She liked the idea of volunteering at a shelter for abused women and children. It seemed like a natural choice. Halle's mother had been a victim of domestic violence, and Halle had struggled as a girl to feel loved and worthy.

Halle was driving home from her first visit at the center when she was hit with a realization. Her question had been answered! In a flash of clarity she saw that she had as much to gain from the women and children at the shelter as they had to gain from her. What's more, Halle found the certainty that all things, no matter how trying, are steps along an unfolding spiritual path.

Must a person ask a question with the intent to answer it in order for that question to help set the stage for an epiphany? A rhetorical question will do, it seems. In the study, fourteen percent of the individuals who asked questions prior to life-changing insights appeared to have posed rhetorical questions.

As Julia Louis-Dreyfus questioned a commitment she had made, she was struck by a pivotal realization. It provided an answer, even though she hadn't seemed interested in finding one.

Julia had actively advocated for the environment. She worked with Heal the Bay, she worked with Heal the Ocean, and she felt good about what she was doing.

Julia and her husband were invited to a dinner party. The hosts were also active in environmental work, and activist Bobby Kennedy Jr. would be among the guests.

As the evening of the party arrived, Julia questioned the decision to attend. She was already an activist. Hadn't she given enough of herself? She was a parent. Shouldn't she stay home on a school night? But Julia and her husband had made a commitment. So they went.

Bobby spoke before dinner. As Julia listened to him, she experienced a powerful epiphany. It showed her how little she had actually done for the environment, and propelled her to do a whole lot more.

Asking questions seemed to set the stage for life-changing insights in many of the accounts in the study, and in some cases rhetorical questions appeared to be sufficient.

▼ ▼ ▼

As for Dayna Smith, she began to follow the doctor's orders after her late-night epiphany. She took her medication and added more fresh fruits and vegetables to her diet. She also exercised several times a week and took steps to manage her stress.

The epiphany had changed how Dayna saw her body. She began to see it as a gift, something to care for.

▼ ▼ ▼

Asking questions can lay the foundation for a pivotal AHA!. Curiosity can draw it forward.

A NOTE TO YOU

What questions do you have about what's happening in your life? What strikes you as curious?

Questions can help set the stage for a momentous insight. Curiosity can coax it along.

Remember to wonder about your current situation.

Notice what's real for you
(It might not be what you think)

As a working mom, Janice Schnake Greene concentrated equally on her career and on her family. She focused her work on teaching others about the environment, and had even received a lifetime service award from the Missouri Environmental Education Association. At home, Janice devoted herself to being the supportive mom of two daughters. She discovered, though, that her best intentions to help weren't always well received.

Amy was in kindergarten and Stephanie in preschool when they began to play YMCA soccer. The girls had a lot of fun—and ate a lot of snacks. As they matured, so did their skills. Soon they joined a competitive league where they trained with paid coaches, practiced twice a week, and traveled to out-of-state tournaments.

Janice enjoyed watching her daughters play. She wanted them to be athletes, something she hadn't had a chance to be when she was growing up. So she committed herself to helping her daughters achieve on the soccer field.

Janice attended the girls' games and cheered from the sideline. Her moment of insight came at one of Stephanie's matches. It was a powerful realization, one that Janice would later describe in an article for *Guideposts* magazine.

Stephanie's team was down a goal and Janice was tense. Then Heather, one of Stephanie's teammates, took possession of the ball and dribbled toward the goal. As the defenders closed in, Janice saw an opening. She shouted to Heather to pass the ball, but Heather continued to dribble. So Janice shouted again—and again.

The shouting upset Heather's mom. "That's it!" she said in disgust as she marched off in a huff. Another mom noticed the commotion and cast a nasty look in Janice's direction.

Surprised by their reactions, Janice felt defensive and unfairly treated. She wasn't a parent with a problem. She didn't belittle the girls. She was just trying to help. It wasn't a big deal, was it? Janice remained lost in thought as the first half ended and the girls took a break.

A whistle signaled that the second half was about to begin. Stephanie trotted back onto the field—her uniform sweaty and stained, her body lean and fit, her focus laser sharp. Janice watched her daughter with admiration. She thought about how Stephanie was becoming the athlete that she had dreamed herself of being. Then she froze, and replayed the thought a second time.

As Janice noticed her thinking, she experienced an AHA!. Suddenly she saw that what she thought was her reason for shouting wasn't her motive at all. Janice had believed that she was just trying to help her daughter and the team. In reality she had been trying to create in Stephanie something she had been unable to achieve for herself.

> *Suddenly she saw that what she thought was her reason for shouting wasn't her motive at all.*

▼ ▼ ▼

A person's reality reflects her perspective on the world. It establishes what's true for her, it determines what's possible for her, and it defines what's important to her. The reality for Janice was that she needed her daughters to become the kind of athletes she had wanted to be, even though she didn't recognize it.

A person's reality might not be what she thinks it is, it might not be what she wants it to be, or it might not be what she wills it to be. And when it's not, noticing the disparity, as Janice did, can help to set the stage for a life-changing epiphany. That held true for fifteen percent of the accounts in the study including those of Cory Booker, Sheryl Lee Ralph, and Mae Jemison.

Cory Booker's reality wasn't what he thought it was. He attended Stanford University on a full football scholarship. He was realistic, knowing that he had little chance of playing professional ball. So he focused on earning a degree and getting into graduate school.

During his senior year Cory played a spectacular game against Notre Dame. Going pro was suddenly an option, and Cory began to plan for a football future. Then he had an AHA! that showed him that he valued service above sports. After that insight he shifted his focus away from a professional football career.

Mae Jemison's reality wasn't what she wanted it to be. She had bought her first house and had a great idea. She could turn a spare bedroom into a dance studio! Although having a studio would be a dream come true, Mae agonized over the decision because the real estate agent had warned her to protect the home's resale value. Mae couldn't figure out why she was intimidated by the agent. She didn't want to be, but she was, even though it was out of character for her.

Years passed without a decision. Then Mae was hit with an insight. She suddenly saw that creating the right home for herself outweighed any resale considerations. The realization netted Mae more than a dance studio. It gave her a new philosophy for living. Sure, it was important to adapt to her circumstances, something she had always been adept at doing. In that moment Mae saw that it was also okay to leave her mark, whether in her home or out in the world.

Sheryl Lee Ralph's reality wasn't what she thought it should be. She had recently gone through a divorce, and when her divorce became final she began to unravel. She couldn't sleep and didn't eat. She doubted herself and became depressed. Her blood pressure began to spike, and she began to lose her hair.

Sheryl gave herself the same advice she had given others who were going through difficult times. She told herself that the real measure of a person was how she responded to life's highs and lows. It was good advice, and she believed it. But it didn't help.

One morning Sheryl had a pivotal realization as she looked closely at herself in the bathroom mirror. She saw that she had strayed from the way she had been raised, which was to be accountable for herself. In that moment Sheryl began to reclaim her life—one step at a time.

Sheryl began to reclaim her life—one step at a time.

In a number of cases in the study, pivotal realizations occurred when people saw that their beliefs about what was true and important didn't match their actions and emotions.

▼ ▼ ▼

As for Janice Schnake Greene, she noticed something as she watched the second half of the soccer game. Heather's mom had returned to the sideline. Janice knew the right thing to do, but just thinking about it made her face flush.

Janice made her way along the edge of the field. The distance was short but the divide was wide. Heather's mom didn't turn to look at Janice—even as the two of them were side by side. Janice apologized and asked for forgiveness. Heather's mom didn't say anything for the longest time. Her eyes focused on the grass. Eventually, she said, "You're right. It was wrong." Janice waited a minute or two, and then walked back to where she had stood.

That evening Janice told Stephanie and Amy what had happened. She apologized and told her daughters that she was proud of them. The girls seemed relieved, thanked their mom, and gave her a big hug.

In the days and weeks that followed, Janice reformed her sideline behavior. She continued to shout at the girls, but only occasionally and only with positives. Other moms noticed the change, and Janice observed ripples from her insight reaching into other areas of her life.

▼ ▼ ▼

What's true and important for a person might not be what that person thinks it is. Noticing the misalignment can spark a pivotal epiphany.

A NOTE TO YOU

What's true and important for you? Don't be surprised if it's not what you think it is.

Observe your reactions. When are they not what you expect them to be? When are they not what you want them to be? When are they not what you will them to be?

Notice what's real for you. (It might not be what you think.)

Be willing to let go

Phil Keoghan has lived a life of adventure. He walked along the wing of a plane in flight. He swam in the largest underwater cave in the world. He fed sharks by hand. These adventures were on Phil's original List for Life. He created that list the day he almost died. It was a day that Phil would later describe in his book, *No Opportunity Wasted*, as well as in an article for *Guideposts* magazine and in numerous interviews with journalists.

At nineteen years old, Phil had landed the dream job of working for an adventure program. When the crew planned to film inside the ballroom of a sunken ship, Phil volunteered to dive—even though he wasn't qualified.

On dive day, Phil was a bundle of nervous energy. He suited up and rolled off the side of the salvage boat. He descended more than a hundred feet and then followed his dive partner into the wreckage. They wound their way through the ship's corridors, eventually arriving at the ballroom where they had to wait for the camera crew. As precious minutes passed, Phil's dive partner motioned to Phil to stay and went in search of the crew.

Alone in the murky space, Phil felt unnerved and abandoned. He didn't know the way out and had no safety line. Despite his efforts to slow his breathing, he began to draw too much air from his tank. He was going to die. He just knew it! As his consciousness faded, he thought about all the things he had dreamed of doing. Now he would never get the chance.

Phil came to on the deck of the salvage boat. He was alive! That moment sparked a pivotal realization for him. He vowed to live life to its fullest, grabbed a paper bag, and wrote his life list on the back. Then he got back to work, diving again to finish the shoot and to check off the first item on his list.

In the weeks and months that followed, Phil continued to add goals to his list, and one by one, he checked them off. Soon he had accomplished almost all of his original targets. He still planned to reach the top of Mount Everest, and he still needed to rocket into outer space.

When Phil became a father ten years later, he read back over his life list. Suddenly he wasn't so interested in climbing the world's highest peak. Was he losing his edge? Was he afraid?

One night as Phil watched his infant daughter sleep, he noticed the innocence of her face and the curve of her fingers. In a flash of insight, he saw that his lack of interest in Mount Everest hadn't come from fear. He hadn't lost his edge, but his responsibilities had changed and so had his priorities.

▼ ▼ ▼

A transformational insight, by definition, exposes the reality of a situation. It uncovers what was previously unseen, misunderstood, or unappreciated. When Phil came to on the deck of the salvage boat, he had an AHA! that showed him the importance of living life to its fullest. Later as a father, he was struck by the realization that he hadn't lost his appetite for adventure but that his priorities had changed.

Sometimes embracing a new reality requires letting go of an

old one. For Phil, embracing the priorities of fatherhood required that he defer his drive for life-and-death adventures.

Forty percent of the accounts in the study included an AHA! that required letting go of something previously known to be true. The stories of Suze Orman, Karen Barber, Edie Falco, and Ty Pennington were included in this group.

Suze Orman's insight required her to let go of her fear of losing her friends. At eight years old, Suze had learned that in order to keep her friends she had to impress them. So she began to steal money from her father to buy them gifts.

A transformational insight, by definition, exposes the reality of a situation.

As an adult Suze tapped her 401(k) and used her credit cards to create the appearance of wealth. She eventually accumulated more than sixty thousand dollars in credit card debt even though she held a well paying job.

Then Suze had a pivotal realization that changed her perspective. She realized that she was living a lie, and she saw that it had caused both her debt and her unhappiness. Once she stopped trying to impress her friends, Suze was able to pay off her debt and build her net worth.

Karen Barber's AHA! meant changing the way she thought about medication. At fifty-four years old, Karen considered herself young and healthy. She was surprised when a routine bone scan revealed osteoporosis. Her doctor wrote a prescription, but Karen kept finding excuses to avoid taking the pills.

Months passed. Then Karen had an epiphany. Suddenly she recognized that she had considered the pills an enemy instead of a gift. With gratitude Karen began to take her medication.

Edie Falco's insight involved thinking about parenthood in a new way. She had wanted to have children but somehow the timing was never quite right. She needed to be ready, she needed to have a man in her life, and she needed to be financially secure.

Edie had just turned forty when she was diagnosed with breast cancer. After eight months of treatment, her doctor declared her cancer free, and Edie had an epiphany. Suddenly she saw that she didn't need to wait to start a family, so she contacted an adoption agency.

Ty Pennington's AHA! required him to see himself differently. At ten years old he was a boy on the move. Forget sitting at a desk—he had too much energy for that. And forget studying—his mind moved way too fast. It was no wonder he struggled in school!

One day Ty noticed that the leg on the family piano had come loose. He knew just what to do. He grabbed his hammer and used it as a lever to work the leg free. He could make good use of that leg.

Ty's mom heard a racket and arrived just in time to divert a disaster. She packed a lunch for her son before pointing him outside. Ty retrieved his toolbox and headed out to the backyard where he had accumulated a pile of cast-off lumber. As he looked at the pile, he pictured an elaborate three-story tree house. Soon he was hard at work.

Hours passed. When Ty finally stepped back for a look, he could barely believe what he had been able to create. And he noticed his mom was impressed too. In a flash of insight, Ty realized that he really was quite capable, despite his struggles in school.

By their nature, pivotal realizations reveal the reality of a situation. Sometimes adopting a new reality requires letting go of a previous one, as was the case in many accounts in the study.

▼ ▼ ▼

As for Phil Keoghan, he continued to add new goals to his life list after his insight—have a barbeque at the South Pole, be a ball boy at the U.S. Open, take his daughter, Elle, to La Tomatina in Spain for the world's biggest food fight.

What happened to climbing Mount Everest? It stayed on the list but was put on hold. While Phil focused on fatherhood, high-risk adventures could wait.

▼ ▼ ▼

Each insight reveals a fresh viewpoint, a startling perspective, or a new reality. Sometimes embracing a new way of seeing things requires letting go of the old.

A NOTE TO YOU

How tightly do you hold on to what you know is true?

An insight will change the way you see a situation. It might even require you to give up something that you thought was indisputable.

Get ready to see things differently.

Be willing to let go.

Watch for Triggers

▼ ▼ ▼

Certain kinds of events tended to trigger profound realizations. You can capitalize on such events to ignite your own pivotal epiphanies. Four triggers in particular point the way.

▼ ▼ ▼

Trigger 1
Catch a glimpse of yourself

Nathan Phillips, a middle school teacher and coach, was up early. Summer was over, and he was headed back to school. As he reached for a pair of pants and pulled them on, he found that they no longer fit. The sixty-eight-inch waistband was too small.

As he eyed his 422-pound body in the mirror, Nathan was struck by an insight. Suddenly he saw just how overweight he was. It was something he hadn't seen before. Not at the doctor's office when the physician prescribed medication for high blood sugar, high cholesterol, and hypertension. Not at the amusement park when people watched and laughed as he tried to squeeze himself into the seat of a roller coaster. Not even at home in bed when the weight of his body made it difficult to breathe and impossible to get a good night's sleep.

People increase their chances of igniting life-changing realizations when they are able to catch a glimpse of themselves.

After his realization Nathan underwent bariatric surgery, changed his eating habits, and began to work out at the gym.

Within two years he had shed 180 pounds—and the need for prescription medication.

People increase their chances of igniting life-changing realizations when they are able to catch a glimpse of themselves. Forty-six percent of the insights in the study arrived this way. It was the most frequent trigger and came in two ways—when people saw themselves clearly and when they saw themselves through the eyes of others.

SEE YOURSELF CLEARLY

Diana Judd grew up in Ashland, Kentucky, along the south bank of the Ohio River. She was a little girl with big aspirations. She wanted to be a star, but her life didn't turn out the way she'd planned. In time Diana would be two thousand miles from home, and even further from her dream.

The countdown to autumn had begun, and in a few days Diana would begin her senior year of high school. It was going to be the best year ever! She just knew it.

One month passed and then two. As Diana marked the time, she held her breath. Her menstrual periods had stopped, and she was petrified to think she might be pregnant. Eventually she made a secret trip to see the doctor. He confirmed her fears.

Abortion wasn't an option. Giving up her baby wasn't an option. Diana considered suicide but couldn't go through with it. Marriage became her only choice. So she and her boyfriend, Michael, stole away to Tennessee—only to discover that at the age of seventeen Diana needed the written permission of her parents to get married. Defeated, the young couple slunk home.

Back in Ashland the two sets of parents took matters into their own hands. A wedding in their hometown church was out of the question, so they were forced to find another alternative. Within days the young couple and their parents made a tense drive to Parisburg, Virginia, for a ceremony that was short and joyless.

Diana and Michael moved in with Michael's parents. Instead of returning to her classes, Diana worked with the school's tutor for homebound students. During graduation week she gave birth to their daughter Christina. Her high school diploma arrived in the mail.

After Michael finished college, the young family relocated to California where their second daughter Ashley was born. Diana adored her girls, but the marriage wasn't a good one. She decided she'd be better off without Michael, so she asked him to leave. The events that followed led Diana to a life-changing epiphany, one that she would later recall in the book *Naomi's Breakthrough Guide*.

Diana struggled to raise two young children alone. Unskilled, she worked minimum-wage jobs, and at times she relied on welfare and food stamps to make ends meet.

> *Diana considered suicide but couldn't go through with it.*

Diana had a boyfriend, but the relationship wasn't working out. So she broke it off. When her enraged ex-boyfriend broke into her home and beat her up, Diana filed charges. The deputy at the sheriff's station warned her to stay away from her house until her ex-boyfriend was taken into custody, but Diana had no money and nowhere to go.

Fortunately, a sympathetic motel clerk gave Diana and her girls a room. Once she was safe inside, Diana surveyed the damage to her face in the bathroom mirror. A black eye. A swollen lip. As she dabbed on makeup to cover up what she could, she wondered how she had ever ended up in such a mess, and then she experienced an insight. "An answer hurled to the surface of my consciousness: *I'd done it all to myself!* Day by day, through the years, I'd kept choosing this dead-end path," she wrote in *Naomi's Breakthrough Guide.*

▼ ▼ ▼

Seeing oneself clearly can trigger a profound AHA!. Such was the case in thirty-four percent of the accounts in the study. Diana found her epiphany as she examined her reflection in a motel mirror, while Kelly Jens experienced her AHA! as she looked at herself in a family photograph.

Kelly had always been passionate about food. When the stay-at-home mom wasn't eating, she was thinking about it. As the years passed, the pounds piled on—especially after two pregnancies.

Christmas had come and gone, complete with family celebrations and pictures. Kelly stared at a holiday photo of herself with her husband and two children. She was startled by what she saw. All 220 pounds of her filled the frame, barely leaving room for her family. In that moment Kelly saw the result for the first time of her fixation on food.

In the days and weeks that followed, Kelly taught herself how to prepare healthy meals. She also began to exercise and started keeping a detailed daily log. Eventually she shed more than ninety pounds and gained the energy to engage actively in her children's lives.

Does it take a glimpse in a mirror or a glance at a photograph to see oneself clearly? The study shows that the answer is no. Only five percent of the pivotal realizations were triggered that way. Instead, seeing oneself clearly usually came when people witnessed their actions, encountered their thoughts, or noticed their emotions, as was the case with Anika Noni Rose, Harry Connick Jr., and Julie Hadden, among others.

Anika Noni Rose had an epiphany as she reached for the phone and felt tears welling up again. She had been out of the country for months filming an HBO series. Exhausted, she had returned home with a stomach flu. For days she didn't move far from her couch, but she couldn't rest. She had things to do that couldn't wait. She knew that if she didn't stay in the public eye she'd be forgotten.

Anika's tears exposed the flaw in her thinking and sparked an insight. In a flash of understanding, she saw that she could relax. She gave herself permission to do what she needed to do for her health and well-being.

As Harry Connick Jr. observed his interactions with his daughter, he had a pivotal realization. He had discovered a small gap in his schedule and decided to take his two-year-old daughter to the park. He hurried her out the door and down the driveway. But the toddler suddenly stopped. Something had caught her eye, and she squatted down to take a closer look. It was a rock!

As precious moments slipped away, Harry urged his daughter to get moving. He rushed her along. He hustled her toward the car. Then he saw what he was doing and experienced an AHA! that transformed his approach to parenting. After that he no longer felt a need to orchestrate his children's lives. Instead, he trusted they would find their way.

> *He no longer felt a need to orchestrate his children's lives. Instead, he trusted they would find their way.*

As Julie Hadden noticed her thinking, she had a life-changing epiphany. At thirty-four years old, Julie packed 218 pounds on her five-foot two-inch frame. She was thrilled when she earned a spot on the reality show *The Biggest Loser*, but during the first week of workouts she clashed with her trainer and was thrown out of the gym. She would be sent home if she couldn't produce a new attitude, and fast.

Back in her room Julie plopped down on the bed and pulled off her sneakers. Psalm 139, her favorite, played across her mind and sparked an insight. Suddenly she realized that she had underestimated herself, and gained the self-respect she needed to succeed.

The next morning Julie was able to convince the trainer that she was ready to return to the gym. She finished the season on the show—enduring extreme workouts, shedding one hundred pounds, and earning the title of Biggest Female Loser of Season Four.

In the study, pivotal epiphanies were often triggered when people saw themselves clearly, which usually involved noticing their thoughts, observing their actions, or recognizing their emotions.

▼ ▼ ▼

As for Diana Judd, after her insight she saw that the life she had been living was out of sync with her values. She eventually moved with her daughters back home to Kentucky and enrolled in nursing school. Later the family of three relocated to Northern California while Diana continued to work on her degree. She attended classes during the day, spent evenings with her girls, and waitressed at night. Along the way Diana changed her name to Naomi and her oldest daughter changed hers to Wynonna.

After graduation Naomi became a registered nurse. She enjoyed her career but still dreamed of being an entertainer. She moved her family again, this time to Nashville, Tennessee. Within a few years she and Wynonna had signed a recording contract with RCA Records.

Naomi and Wynonna called their duo *The Judds*. They went on to sell twenty million albums, have fifteen number-one hits, and earn sixty music industry awards.

▼ ▼ ▼

Seeing one's self clearly can be educational. It can also spark a pivotal realization.

A NOTE TO YOU

*How well do you know yourself?
Don't be surprised if it's not as well as you think.*

Notice what you do.

Pay attention to what you think.

Be aware of your feelings.

As you discover more about yourself, you might spark an epiphany.

Be alert. Be attentive. See yourself clearly.

SEE YOURSELF THROUGH
THE EYES OF OTHERS

"Do something of service," Bob Curry often said to his five children, and they listened. While his two sons followed him into the military, his oldest daughter Ann became a journalist. It took her many years though to discover how she could truly be of service, as she would later recount in an article for *Guideposts* magazine.

Ann had attended the University of Oregon. Money was tight.

So she clerked in a bookstore, made maps for the U.S. Forest Service, and cleaned rooms in a hotel. In 1978 Ann graduated with a degree in journalism, and she landed a job—as a cocktail waitress.

During college Ann had worked as an intern at KTVL, a television station in Medford, Oregon. So when a reporter's job opened up there, Ann applied for the position. The station had never had a female reporter, and the hiring producer told Ann that women weren't capable of performing the job.

Ann didn't have any hope of winning the job at KTVL, but she thought about what her father had said about service. She also remembered what her mother had said about persistence.

Ann's mother had grown up on a rice farm in Japan. "Gambaru," she would often tell her children and then remind them of the word's meaning: "Never ever give up, even and especially when there's no chance of winning."

> *"Never ever give up, even and especially when there's no chance of winning."*

Ann didn't give up. She eventually persuaded the KTVL producer to hire her and began steadily to advance in her career. In 1981 she moved to Portland, Oregon, to join KGW, and in 1984 she took a job with KCBS in Los Angeles.

In L.A., Ann often covered breaking news, winning Emmy Awards for her coverage of an earthquake and of a pipeline explosion. But it was a human-interest piece about a little boy with a birth defect that was the most memorable for her.

Unable to use his thumb because it was fused to his hand, the boy was tormented by the taunts of other children. Corrective surgery was out of the question. The boy's parents had neither the insurance to cover it nor the funds to pay for it.

Ann's story on the boy sparked a chain of events. A nurse watched the broadcast on the local news. She contacted a surgeon, and together they devised a plan to provide the operation at no charge.

After the surgery Ann joined the boy and his family in the recovery room. The boy beamed as he showed Ann his hand and thanked her. In that instant, Ann realized the potential of her position. She recognized a double opportunity—to provide exposure for people who were suffering and to give viewers the chance to care.

▼ ▼ ▼

People can learn plenty by observing themselves from the vantage point of others. What do other people see when they look at them? How do they respond to what they say? How do they react to what they do?

Seeing oneself through the eyes of others can also ignite life-changing epiphanies. That was the case in twelve percent of the accounts in the study.

> *People can learn plenty by observing themselves from the vantage point of others.*

In a quarter of this subset, AHA!s were sparked when a person interacted with a family member or an acquaintance. For Ron Blomberg it was his wife. For Josh Hamilton it was his grandmother, and for Norman Vincent Peale it was his professor.

In the remaining seventy-five percent of the subset, insights were triggered when people interfaced with individuals with whom they had little, if any, prior contact. Ann Curry, Alfre Woodard, Patricia Cardoso, and Bil Cornelius were included in this category.

When Alfre Woodard traveled to Africa to shoot the movie *Mandela*, the reactions of the locals to her appearance sparked a pivotal realization for her. When it came to her looks, Alfre had always found it hard to satisfy others. When she was growing up, her mother told her she was pretty, but kids teased her and nicknamed her "Bubble Lips" and "Frog Eyes."

As an adult, Alfre moved to Hollywood to pursue an acting career. In auditions she frequently found that her features weren't a fit for the roles. She looked too African, she was told.

Then Alfre traveled to Zimbabwe to film *Mandela*. There the locals raved about her beauty, and their reaction sparked a pivotal realization. It led her to embrace her appearance and to recognize that she could serve as a role model for women back home.

When Patricia Cardoso was a graduate student, the positive reaction of professors to her work triggered an insight for her.

Patricia knew next to nothing about creating films, but she thought it would make a good career. After earning a Fulbright scholarship, she enrolled in the filmmaking program at the University of California, Los Angeles.

In her second year at UCLA, Patricia hoped to take a film-editing course. The professors were highly respected. One of them had even been nominated three times for an Academy Award. The professors were also known for their selectivity and high standards, requiring that each student apply for the course by submitting a film for review.

Application day arrived. Patricia showed her film, and then she waited nervously through the silence that followed. They must hate it, she thought. But the professors loved her film! Their praise of her work sparked an insight for Patricia that gave her confidence in her career.

Bil Cornelius didn't need to witness the reactions of others in order to experience a pivotal realization. All he had to do was to imagine their perspective.

Bil had caught a glimpse of a photograph of himself and his wife with another couple. He was startled at how overweight he looked. He blamed a bad angle and told his wife not to show the picture to anyone.

Then Bil realized that hiding the photo wouldn't solve his problem. People saw the same Bil any time they looked at him—whether in person or in a picture. That AHA! gave Bil the motivation he needed to change his eating habits, start exercising, and slim down.

In the study epiphanies were triggered when people saw themselves through the eyes of others. These insights occurred in a range of interactions, both real and imagined, with family members, acquaintances, and strangers.

▼ ▼ ▼

As for Ann Curry, she continued to report the news. She moved to Chicago to become an NBC correspondent in 1990. The next year she became a news anchor, first on *NBC News at Sunrise* and later on the *Today Show*.

After her AHA! Ann felt an urgency to report on the hardships that people faced. She traveled to the far reaches of the world to log reports—even after becoming an anchor. "My aim," Ann said in a 2010 commencement speech at Wheaton College, "is to reveal the truth about war, genocide, crimes against humanity, and other human suffering."

▼ ▼ ▼

Observing yourself through the eyes of others can be informative. It can also trigger a pivotal realization.

A NOTE TO YOU

What do others recognize in you that you don't see in yourself?

As you pay attention to how people react to you, you might trigger a powerful AHA!.

Be observant.

See yourself through the eyes of others.

Trigger 2
Catch a glimpse of others

Hope Davis set off with her family for a Maine vacation. Little did she know that she was about to experience a life-changing realization—one she would later describe in an interview with Justine van der Leun for *O, The Oprah Magazine.*

Hope and her husband, Jon, had left their two young daughters in the care of Hope's sister while they went for an evening out. They enjoyed dinner and a movie and then headed back to the vacation cottage. Jon, who was driving, spotted a shortcut and made a quick turn. Hope and Jon were so deep in their conversation that

> *Little did she know that she was about to experience a life-changing realization.*

they didn't even notice they had passed a young woman on the street. They didn't notice, that is, until they heard her shout, "This is a one-way street, *you asshole!*"

Hope was furious at the woman's attitude. Jon wasn't. He stopped the car, smiled, and said hello. He apologized and told the woman that he hadn't seen the sign. The woman calmed down, pointed to the sign, and agreed that it wasn't very visible.

She said she was sorry, too. Then Jon and the woman wished each other well as they went their separate ways.

As Hope watched that interaction between her husband and the woman, she experienced an epiphany. Suddenly she saw just how inaccurate hasty judgments could be. The young woman had seen Jon and Hope as self-absorbed tourists, while Hope had seen the woman as a bitter local. As it turned out, neither was correct. That insight stayed with Hope in the days and weeks that followed, giving her greater patience with people.

Glimpsing a new view of others triggered life-changing realizations in twenty-five percent of the accounts in the study. The discoveries came in two ways—seeing others clearly and understanding their perspective.

SEE OTHERS CLEARLY

Sela Ward grew up in Meridian, Mississippi—a land of red clay, sweet tea, and unwavering courtesy. She enjoyed life in her small Southern town. Yet she was drawn to places far away. It would take Sela many years to recognize that, regardless of where she lived, Meridian would always be home. As she reconnected with her roots, Sela experienced an insight. She would later describe that insight and its impact in her book, *Homesick: A Memoir*, and in articles for *O, The Oprah Magazine* and *Guideposts* magazine.

As high school came to an end, most of Sela's friends chose in-state colleges. Sela didn't. Instead she enrolled at the University of Alabama where she majored in art and communications and was a Crimson Tide cheerleader. When the basketball team played in Madison Square Garden, Sela fell in love—with New York City. She promised herself she'd live there someday.

After college and a job that didn't work out, Sela met a man on a plane who promised her a job in Manhattan if she ever were to live there. A casual conversation and the word of a stranger were enough for her. She moved—and was hired as an illustrator.

Sela soon discovered that her modest paycheck wouldn't cover the bills. Her mother urged her to move back home, but Sela stayed in New York. She went into modeling at the suggestion of a friend and later took up acting.

Los Angeles seemed to Sela to be a better place to launch an acting career. So she moved—and landed work in addition to meeting her future husband, Howard.

After the wedding, Sela felt a shift. As she thought about the children she hoped to have, she felt the urge to give them a Southern home. Within months Sela and Howard had purchased property near Meridian and set about making it their own. Sela experienced the joy a few years later of introducing their son, Austin, and then their daughter, Anabella, to their Mississippi home away from home.

It was almost Christmas. Sela, Howard, and their children did what they always did at that time of year. They dropped what they were doing in L.A. and headed home to Meridian.

In her hometown, Sela stopped to visit a friend who had founded a shelter for abused children. She chatted with her friend, took a tour of the building, and asked about the children's Christmas wishes.

Sela returned to the shelter a few days later. She balanced an armload of presents as she stepped onto the porch and through the front door. While she stacked the presents under the Christmas tree, she noticed two young boys standing along the wall, brothers who had just arrived at the shelter. She smiled at the boys and wished them a Merry Christmas. "Merry Christmas, ma'am," said the older boy, while the younger one smiled shyly.

The boys are so precious, thought Sela. They have such potential. As they melted Sela's heart, they sparked a pivotal insight for her. "They're part of my family too, of my community, my town," she said in a *Guideposts* article.

▼ ▼ ▼

Taking notice of others and catching a clear view of them can be instructive. Discovering the essence, the character, and the spirit of another can also ignite a significant AHA!. That was the case in eight percent of the accounts in the study including those of Sela, Lenedra Carroll, and Gail Buckley.

Lenedra Carroll had a pivotal epiphany when she caught a clear view of an adversary. She managed the singing career of her daughter, Jewel. In one meeting, Lenedra talked with a booking agent who was determined to schedule Jewel for an event. He applied pressure, tried to intimidate Lenedra, and made threats.

> *Discovering the essence, the character, and the spirit of another can also ignite a significant AHA!.*

Lenedra was afraid. Then she wondered if she could see the situation differently. As she asked herself some questions and looked the rep in the eye, she was struck by an insight. He was just a regular guy pretending to be a shark! She stifled a giggle and relaxed. In that instant she gained a new perspective that gave her a productive approach for handling menacing personalities.

For Gail Buckley, a close-up look at her ancestors sparked a powerful AHA!. She had inherited a well-worn travel trunk that had once belonged to her grandfather. She put the trunk in her basement, and there it sat forgotten for almost twenty years.

When Gail decided to declutter her house, she knew that the old trunk had to go. She almost threw it away without opening it, but opted to take a peek in honor of her grandfather. What she found in the trunk was a rich family history dating back to the mid-1800s. The discovery sparked an insight for her. There had been a black middle class in America in the nineteenth and early twentieth centuries! It was a narrative that had been of little interest to the media. But Gail knew that the story was important and needed to be told, which she did in her well-received book *The Hornes: An American family.*

Catching a clear view of others wasn't limited to observations of humans. Mary Tyler Moore and Octavia Butler experienced powerful insights during interactions with animals.

Mary Tyler Moore had a momentous epiphany as she looked into the eyes of a spotted cow. She adored animals and had long lobbied for their humane treatment. During visits to her country home, she savored quiet walks with her husband past pastures of horses, sheep, and cattle.

On one springtime stroll, Mary noticed a cow standing by a fence, chewing her cud. Mary drew close, but the cow didn't shy away. As Mary looked into the cow's eyes, she experienced an AHA!. It gave her an even greater respect for animals and prompted her to become a vegetarian.

Octavia Butler had a pivotal AHA! as she studied the household dog. Octavia's father had died the year she was born. To support the family, her mother had taken a job as a live-in maid.

One day Octavia, who was not quite three, sat face to face in the hallway with Baba, the employer's cocker spaniel. As Octavia gazed at him, he gazed at her. As she studied him, he studied her. As she got to know him, he got to know her.

The interaction with Baba sparked an epiphany that Octavia carried into adulthood. It showed her the importance of looking into the eyes of others and discovering who they truly are.

Catching a clear view of others sparked life-changing insights in several accounts in the study, and in half of those cases observing the eyes of others was important to generating the AHA!s.

▼ ▼ ▼

As for Sela, after her insight she told Howard about the boys at the shelter and described the feelings they stirred in her. She also told him the boys would probably be sent to separate foster homes. She asked Howard what he thought the two of them could do to help.

Howard suggested that they create a permanent home for the boys and other children without families. It would be a place where kids could live safely, find stability until they were eighteen, and learn practical skills.

Sela and Howard soon found the perfect spot in Meridian—a vacant building on twenty-five acres. But they needed to raise funds to buy the property and to renovate the structure. Sela contacted a friend at the Entertainment Industry Foundation, and the friend made arrangements for Sela to appear in Kentucky Fried Chicken ads in exchange for an endowment. Before long, Hope Village opened its doors to forty children in need of a home.

▼ ▼ ▼

Catching a clear view of others, especially their eyes, can trigger a life-changing epiphany.

A NOTE TO YOU

*How well do you know others?
Don't be surprised if it's not as well
as you think.*

*Be observant. Take a close look. Notice
their eyes.*

*As you see things about them that you
haven't seen before, you could ignite
an AHA!.*

Catch a clear view of others.

UNDERSTAND THE PERSPECTIVE OF OTHERS

Gary Hirshberg was raised in the White Mountains of New Hampshire. He came from a family of industrialists. His father manufactured shoes and so did his grandfather. But as he was growing up, Gary saw the negative effects of commercialism on the environment, on *his* environment and the land that he loved. He vowed never to go into business. Eventually, though, he realized he was making a strategic mistake. He would later describe that epiphany in his book *Stirring It Up* and in an article for *Newsweek*.

In college Gary had majored in ecology, and his studies increased his sense of alarm about the environment. After graduation, he took a job as executive director of the New Alchemy Institute, an ecological research and education center.

The institute staff devised a greenhouse that was a model for sustainability. They used large tanks of water to raise schools of fish, and to capture the sun's rays to heat the building. They fertilized the plants with the waste of the fish, and fed the fish using some of the plants. They used wind turbines to generate power for the structure.

The greenhouse had the capacity to feed ten people year round—all without fossil fuels, insecticides, herbicides, or chemical-based fertilizers. Gary and his colleagues were excited about the potential of what they had created.

Gary's mother worked in Florida for the Walt Disney Company. When Gary visited in 1982, he and his mother toured EPCOT Center, a theme park focused on the advancements of technology and the cultures of the world. They stopped at the Land Pavilion, which demonstrated the future of farming—at least from the view of Kraft Foods, the pavilion's sponsor. But Gary found the exhibit to be bizarre and disturbing—the antithesis of everything he had worked so hard to create at the New Alchemy Institute. He noticed the crowd around him and performed a quick calculation. More people visited the Land Pavilion in one day than toured the institute in an entire year.

While brooding over his experience, Gary was hit with an insight and said aloud, "I have to become Kraft!" In that moment he understood that he needed the clout of a successful business to get the attention of others and to convince them to change. It was the source of real hope for the planet.

▼ ▼ ▼

How do others react to a situation? What do they believe? How do they view the world around them? Understanding the perspective of others can ignite a powerful AHA!, which was the case in seventeen percent of the accounts in the study.

A person didn't need to agree with another's opinion in order for that outlook to spark an epiphany. Gary saw how the EPCOT audience valued the viewpoint of Kraft. He thought otherwise. Yet, understanding the standpoint of others triggered a transformational insight for him.

Gary was not alone. Wanda Sykes, Camelia Entekhabi-Fard, and Christy Turlington were among those in the study who disagreed with the perspectives that led to their pivotal realizations.

Wanda Sykes had a powerful AHA! as she understood her husband's point of view. When she and her husband had decided to separate, the timing couldn't have been worse. She had just one week to finish fine-tuning her comedy act before flying to Los Angeles to perform on Comedy Central.

> *Understanding the perspective of others can ignite a powerful AHA!.*

Wanda took the break up hard—and took it on the road, weaving stories of her troubled relationship into her standup routine. Although Wanda had always been rather honest in her act, she had never before used material from her marriage.

The day of the Comedy Central performance arrived. The routine went well, and afterwards Wanda went out to celebrate with friends. Suddenly her husband's perspective pierced her mind. In that moment Wanda realized that she preferred to live alone rather than under the constant cloud of her husband's criticism. The insight gave Wanda the freedom to relax and to be herself—on stage and in her relationships.

An insight struck Camelia Entekhabi-Fard when she saw the perspective of governmental officials in her home country of Iran. She had begun working as a reporter in Tehran while she was still a teenager. As a person known to think independently and speak frankly, she loved her job. It was her life, and marriage could wait.

When Camelia was twenty years old, the Iranian government shuttered *Zan*, the reformist newspaper where she worked. She was in the United States at the time. Her mother and others warned her not to come home. Camelia ignored their advice and returned to Tehran temporarily to gather information for a story. Within days she was imprisoned on charges of spying for the Israelis.

Weeks passed. Camelia sat in solitary confinement trying to decipher the true reason for her detainment. In a flash of clarity, she found her answer, seeing that her government expected her to be a wife and mother first and foremost. Camelia knew that to remain true to herself she would need to emigrate at the first opportunity, and she did.

> *In a flash of clarity, she found her answer.*

Christy Turlington had a momentous realization when she noticed a prevailing perception in the modeling industry. She had recently managed to quit smoking, a marvelous thing for her health. She had gained a few pounds as a result but didn't give it much thought. Shortly after quitting, she flew to Paris to model in the haute couture fashion shows.

After a fitting for Yves Saint Laurent, Christy's agent told her that she had lost her spot in that show. Later, she even heard a rumor that she might be pregnant. As she noticed how others were reacting to her body, she had an epiphany. Suddenly she saw the misalignment between her values and those of the modeling industry, and she decided to retire from the runway.

Gary, Wanda, Camelia, and Christy were among those who disagreed with the perspectives that sparked their insights, but they were in the minority. In fifty-nine percent of the cases in this subset, individuals resonated with the viewpoints that triggered their insights. That held true for Blair Underwood and Marcia Gay Harden, among others.

An AHA! hit Blair Underwood when he understood his fiancée's point of view. While he and his fiancée, Desiree, were driving home from an evening out, Desiree began to describe a difficult challenge she was facing. As Blair listened, he did what he learned from his father to do when something was broken. He tried to fix Desiree's situation.

Desiree patiently explained that she wasn't looking to him for a solution and that she simply needed to confide in him. As he understood his fiancée's viewpoint, he experienced an insight that enriched his relationship with the women in his life—Desiree, his mother, and his sisters.

Marcia Gay Harden had an epiphany when she understood the viewpoint of a homeless man. She had moved to New York City to pursue a career in acting. Months passed, winter arrived, and half-melted snow puddled at every street corner. Marcia sobbed as she made her way down Broadway. Her feet were soaked, she had a fever, and she hadn't landed a single role.

A homeless man fell in step with her and asked what was wrong. She told him. Did she have a job, the man asked. Did she have a place to live? Did she have family who cared about her? She did. In that case, the man suggested, she should stop complaining and press on. The homeless man's perspective triggered a pivotal realization for Marcia. It vaporized her self-pity and replaced it with gratitude—not only in that moment but also in the months and years that followed.

Understanding the viewpoint of others triggered pivotal insights in a number of accounts in the study, whether or not the person who had the epiphany resonated with the perspective.

▼ ▼ ▼

As for Gary Hirshberg, he partnered with Samuel Kaymen to found Stonyfield Farm. They began making organic yogurt with "seven cows and a dream." A drafty, ramshackle farmhouse served as the company's offices, the yogurt factory, and living quarters for the men and their families.

Gary and Samuel struggled to create a viable enterprise. They dodged calamity. They held off bankruptcy. They persevered. In 1992 Stonyfield Farm earned a profit, and in 1999 its annual sales surpassed the yogurt sales of Kraft Foods.

▼ ▼ ▼

Understanding another person's perspective can be illuminating. It can also trigger a pivotal AHA!.

A NOTE TO YOU

What do you notice about the viewpoints of others?

Pay attention to how people react. Notice what they believe. Uncover their worldviews.

Whether you agree with them or not, you might ignite an insight.

Understand the perspective of others.

Trigger 3
Follow the lead
of your VIPs

Kerry Washington was serious about acting, so she majored in theater at George Washington University. She also maintained a flawless figure, knowing that she had to if she hoped to make it as an actress.

Things changed after Kerry graduated. Food made her feel better. So she ate, and the result was reflected on the scale as Kerry gained five, ten, and then fifteen pounds. She was afraid that her career was over, but she continued to audition anyway.

Kerry was surprised to land a starring role in *Our Song*, a full-length movie. As rehearsals began, the director cautioned Kerry not to lose weight. She was lovely and just right for the role, he assured her. As Kerry listened to the director's comment, she was struck by an insight that delivered self-acceptance and dissolved her drive for perfection.

Following the lead of one's VIPs (Very Important People) sparked life-changing realizations in fourteen percent of the accounts in the study. Those realizations came in two ways—hearing what VIPs said and watching what they did. In some situations, though, following the lead of a VIP wasn't a good fit. Even then, interactions with VIPs helped set the stage for powerful AHA!s.

HEAR WHAT YOUR VIPS ARE SAYING

"Honey, this is only a moment. It's not the rest of your life." Julianna Margulies had often heard her mother say those words, but she never quite figured out what her mother meant—until one night when she really needed the advice.

"Honey, this is only a moment. It's not the rest of your life."

In that moment her mother's words sparked a life-changing insight for Julianna—one she would later recall in an interview with Suzan Colón for *O, The Oprah Magazine.*

Julianna had played the role of nurse Carol Hathaway on the medical drama *ER* for seven years. After leaving the show in 2000, Julianna worked on a number of projects in a variety of places, and in 2006 she began to focus on finding projects based in New York City, her hometown.

An opportunity arose the next year for Julianna to play the lead role in *Canterbury's Law*, a legal drama on the Fox network. She was thrilled that the series would be filmed in New York City, she loved the Elizabeth Canterbury character, and she would have a handy legal consultant in Keith, her soon-to-be husband, an attorney. Despite all the positives, Julianna hesitated to sign on, knowing that the filming schedule for a network series would be grueling. She took time to weigh the decision and eventually opted in.

When the cast and crew began shooting early episodes of the show, Julianna stepped easily into the role. There was one challenge, though. She was pregnant, a fact that became increasingly difficult to hide as shooting progressed.

When baby Kieran was born, Julianna took time off to be with him. After six months she returned to work, having landed the role of Joyce Rizzo in the movie *City Island*. Days on the set were long. Evenings at home were short. Julianna was tired.

One evening Keith was out of town and Julianna was home alone with Kieran. At 2:00 a.m. the baby awoke crying. No matter how Julianna tried to soothe him, he wouldn't calm down.

Julianna needed to be at work by 6:00 a.m. She worried about losing precious sleep, arriving late to the set, and feeling exhausted. The more she thought about her predicament, the more distraught she became.

Then her mother's voice played through her mind. "Honey, this is only a moment. It's not the rest of your life." In a flash of clarity Julianna understood for the first time what those words meant.

▼ ▼ ▼

A person can gain a lot by listening to personal VIPs. It's an opportunity to appreciate a new perspective, to find comfort, and to accumulate wisdom. Hearing, really hearing, what one's VIPs are saying can also trigger a pivotal realization. That was the case in eight percent of the accounts in the study.

Young Julianna heard the same advice from her mother over and over. Yet she was a mom herself before an insight revealed the meaning of her mother's words.

Bernie Mac experienced a similar situation with his mom. "Always give your best," she had often told him. Yet Bernie was an adult and a father before he had an AHA! that revealed the wisdom of his mother's words.

It took years for Julianna and Bernie to understand the advice they received from their mothers, but they were in the minority.

In sixty-three percent of the cases in this subset, hearing the advice of a VIP the first time was sufficient to spark a momentous epiphany. That held true for Michael Romano, Angela Bassett, and Maria Bello, among others.

A comment made by a prominent chef sparked an AHA! for Michael Romano. As a young man Michael didn't know what he

A comment made by a prominent chef sparked an AHA! for Michael Romano.

wanted to do with his life. So he worked in a Manhattan restaurant, deflected pressure from his parents to get an office job, and tried to figure things out. When the owner of the restaurant saw that Michael had an interest in cooking, he arranged for him to meet James Beard—t*he* James Beard who was once dubbed the "Dean of American Cookery" by *The New York Times.*

Michael met with James Beard in his West Village apartment. During their conversation Mr. Beard told Michael that he could make a career out of cooking. The comment triggered an insight for Michael that expanded his perception of what was possible and convinced him to become a chef.

For Angela Bassett, an interaction with her mother ignited an epiphany. Angela had always made the honor roll. It was what her mother expected, nothing less. One marking period Angela earned a "C." She knew that her mother would be upset and built a case to justify the grade. She told her mother that a "C" meant that she was average, and that there was nothing wrong with that.

Angela's mother didn't budge. *Her* kids weren't average, she told her daughter. The comment sparked an insight for Angela that increased her self-confidence and propelled her to perform.

For Maria Bello, a conversation with her college mentor triggered an AHA!. As a freshman at Villanova University, she had taken a course in peace and justice education. Father Ray Jackson taught the course, became Maria's mentor, and played a part in her decision to become a human rights lawyer.

In her junior year, though, Maria took a course in acting and was hooked. She wanted to change career paths but worried about disappointing Father Ray. After all, what kind of positive impact could she make on the world as an actor?

Maria described her dilemma to Father Ray. He assured her that people contribute the most when they do what they love. His response ignited an epiphany for Maria that cemented her decision to pursue a new profession.

In the study, profound AHA!s were triggered when people heard what their VIPs were saying, whether the message was brand new or quite familiar.

▼ ▼ ▼

As for Julianna, her perception of her predicament changed after her insight. As she relaxed, so did her infant son. Soon he fell asleep, and so did she.

Julianna made it to work the next day. Sure, she was tired but the day wasn't the catastrophe she had imagined it would be.

As months and years went by, Julianna focused on living in the moment. At times she would forget and get caught up in the tension of trying to make things happen. When she did, she'd remind herself of her mother's wisdom.

▼ ▼ ▼

Hearing what VIPs are saying can be educational, and it can spark a momentous insight.

A NOTE TO YOU

What are the VIPs in your life telling you?

Pay attention to their perspective. Consider their words of wisdom.

As you listen to them, you might trigger a pivotal realization.

Hear what your VIPs are saying.

NOTICE WHAT YOUR VIPS ARE DOING

Fiona Apple released her first album, *Tidal,* in 1996 and became an overnight sensation. The following year she was named Best New Artist at the MTV Video Music awards. Her days became a whirl of tours, interviews, and negotiations with the record company. Instead of enjoying the success, Fiona was traumatized by her new life. She was stressed, she was scared, and she felt misunderstood.

In 2000 Fiona walked away from her work. She spent most of her days sitting alone in her large, secluded yard thinking, meditating, and trying to figure things out. Every Tuesday Fiona would have lunch with Jon Brion, her friend and producer. He would encourage her to work, but she would resist.

In early 2002 Jon coaxed Fiona back into the studio, and they recorded eleven songs, calling the new album *Extraordinary Machine.* Fiona was proud of what they had created. But she didn't think the songs were ready to be released, and she wanted to keep working on them—to experiment and re-record them.

Fiona approached Epic Records for additional funding. She understood that the company would finance the rework *only* if they had final say over the album's contents. Fiona couldn't bear to sign away her creative freedom. She pulled the plug on the project and retreated once again.

Little did Fiona know that a chain of events would spark a momentous epiphany, one that would send her back into the recording studio. It was an experience that she would later recall in an article for *O, The Oprah Magazine* and in several interviews.

In the summer of 2004 songs from *Extraordinary Machine* mysteriously began to appear on the Internet. By early 2005 the complete album was on the Web, but Fiona ignored the leak and the entire music industry.

At the time Fiona was visiting her mother in Manhattan. It was there where she had learned to play the piano when she was a child. It was there where she had read the poems of Maya Angelou and written her own. And it was there where she had worried she'd never have friends who understood her, who cared about her, and who missed her when she wasn't around.

Fiona spent her days stretched out on her mom's sofa, wearing pajamas without bothering to change. She watched reruns of Columbo on television while contemplating her life's direction.

One afternoon Fiona's manager called to tell her that her fans were furious. They thought that Epic Records had refused to release the album, and they had organized a Free Fiona campaign. They were holding rallies outside the corporate office and flooding the company with apples, apple stickers, apple drawings, and other apple items.

Fiona immediately recognized the irony in what was happening. Her fans were hard at work while she was lounging around. She laughed, hung up the phone, and went online to learn more about what her fans were doing. Then she thought about her childhood fear of never finding friends, and her laughter gave way to tears as she was struck by a flash of clarity. "If somebody wants me in the room, I realized, I had better show up," she recounted in *O, The Oprah Magazine*.

▼ ▼ ▼

Noticing what one's VIPs are doing can be educational. It can also spark a profound AHA!, which was the case in six percent of the accounts in the study.

Fiona didn't need to witness what her fans were doing to trigger a pivotal insight. Simply learning about their actions was enough for her. Was her experience unusual? Wouldn't profound realizations more likely come from first-hand observations of VIPs? The answer, based on the study sample, is no. The accounts were evenly divided between those who witnessed the actions of their VIPs, such as Holly Robinson Peete and Lucille Ball, and those who heard or read about what their VIPs had done, such as Fiona and Melina Kanakaredes.

Noticing what one's VIPs are doing can spark a profound AHA!.

Watching a VIP on television sparked an epiphany for Holly Robinson Peete. She adored her father and had just started college in the fall of 1982 when she learned that he had been diagnosed with Parkinson's disease. He was forty-six years old. There was no cure.

Holly stood helplessly by as her father's condition worsened. In 1996 she watched the opening ceremony of the Summer Olympics on television. She watched as Muhammad Ali held the Olympic flame, standing tall despite the tremors he suffered from Parkinson's. As Holly observed his courage, she experienced an insight that gave her hope and prompted her to create a foundation to help people who had been diagnosed with the disease.

Lucille Ball was struck by an AHA! as she watched the performance of a popular celebrity. It was a moment that she would later recall in a conversation with Charles Higham, author of the biography *Lucy: The real life of Lucille Ball*.

In 1923 when Lucy was not yet a teenager, her parents took her to see a famous comedian of that era, Julius Tannen. He sat alone on the stage wearing a tailored suit and pince nez glasses. He enthralled the audience with his mock somberness, hilarious stories, and flawless timing. As Lucy watched, she experienced an epiphany that showed her the transfixing power of a performance and opened her eyes to the possibility of a career as an actress and comedienne. "He changed my life," she told Higham. "I knew it was a very serious, wonderful thing to be able to make people laugh and cry."

Melina Kanakaredes experienced a powerful insight when she learned about her grandfather's struggles. She had always admired her grandfather. He had immigrated to the United States as a teenager, started a candy company in the basement of his Akron, Ohio, home, and taught Melina to embrace her Greek heritage.

Melina was devastated when her grandfather died, and it was then that she learned of the monumental challenges he had faced in his life. She reflected on what her grandfather had been able to accomplish despite the many setbacks he faced, and she experienced an epiphany. It gave her the confidence to be herself and the resolve to follow her dreams.

In the study, momentous epiphanies were triggered when people noticed what their VIPs were doing, whether the VIP actions were witnessed directly or learned about secondhand.

▼ ▼ ▼

As for Fiona, she got back to work after her AHA!. She asked the record company for funding and for the freedom to create, and won agreement. She began to experiment with the songs on the unfinished album, changing all but two of the original recordings. Within the year, *Extraordinary Machine* was released and was nominated for a Grammy Award.

After her insight, Fiona let go of her fears. "When that happens," she told Jenny Eliscu in an interview for *Rolling Stone*, "you can play a little bit more and you can be looser and not worry about falling down so much because you know that, whatever happens, you're going to be OK."

▼ ▼ ▼

Observing the actions of one's VIPs can be helpful. Doing so can also ignite a life-changing insight.

A NOTE TO YOU

Who are your VIPs? How are they role models for you?

Pay attention to the values they exemplify. Notice the standards they set.

As you watch your VIPs in action, you might spark an epiphany.

Notice what your VIPs are doing.

BEWARE OF WHAT'S NOT A FIT FOR YOU

As a teenager, Angela Bassett fell in love with acting. She decided to major in theater in college, but a well-meaning aunt convinced her otherwise.

In high school Angela had stayed busy. She joined the cheerleading squad. She studied just enough to stay on the honor roll, and she hung out with friends—the nerdy ones, the religious ones, the artsy ones, *and* the popular ones.

Angela also participated in the Upward Bound program in her hometown of St. Petersburg, Florida. The program brought teenagers together from across the city to sharpen their academic skills and to broaden their cultural understanding. The goal was to get the students into colleges and to prepare them to succeed there.

The Upward Bound director selected Angela to travel to Washington, D.C., to attend the Presidential Classroom for Young Americans. Little did Angela know that her experience in Washington would lead to a momentous realization—one that she would describe many years later in her book, *Friends, A Love Story*.

The Presidential Classroom program included a week of activities focused on government and politics, but Angela spent the time half listening. She was more interested in the upcoming sightseeing tours. One evening the group went to the Kennedy Center to see the play *Of Mice and Men*. Angela sat in the audience, her eyes riveted to the stage as she watched the story unfold and the tension mount. When the play hit its climax, she dissolved into tears.

The performance ended, and the theater emptied. Angela lingered in her seat. Still in tears, she wondered how everyone else so easily could just stand up and go home. Then she had an AHA!.

She wanted to be able to impact others in the same way that the performance had impacted her, and she decided to pursue a career on stage.

Back home, Angela got to work. She joined the high school drama society, performed at church, and participated in the arts evenings at Upward Bound. She would eventually lose sight of her dream but then find it again through another insight. It was an insight that she would later describe in an interview with Naomi Barr for *O, The Oprah Magazine.*

When Angela graduated from high school, she enrolled in Yale University. The university intimidated her, but she soon discovered that she could rise to the academic challenge. So she settled into a routine. She acted—doing plays every semester. She partied—kicking off most weekends on Wednesday night. And, she studied—squeezing in academics by pulling all nighters.

She would eventually lose sight of her dream but then find it again through another insight.

Angela had planned to major in theater, but her aunt had other ideas. Aunt Golden told Angela that she should focus on something practical. Angela respected her aunt a great deal, and besides, Aunt Golden was the only person in the family who had gone to college. So instead of theater, Angela decided to major in administrative science.

By her junior year, Angela was struggling. She was in danger of failing one of her courses. She had to do something. So she decided to forgo the stage and concentrate on her studies. When she noticed that she was still staying up all night to cram for her courses, she had another epiphany. "It was as if the final piece of the puzzle presented itself and everything became clear," Angela told Barr. Suddenly she saw that a lack of passion was her problem and made plans to focus on the work that she loved.

▼ ▼ ▼

Aunt Golden had meant well. She wanted only the best for her niece, but her advice wasn't a good fit for Angela.

Following the lead of a VIP sparked pivotal AHA!s in fourteen percent of the accounts in the study. But in eight percent of the accounts following the lead of a VIP proved to be problematic, as was the case for Angela. In each of these cases, though, an AHA! put the person back on track. Shonda Rhimes, Jill Scott, and Chitra Banerjee Divakaruni were also among those included in this group.

Shonda Rhimes was in a bind. She was holding herself to a standard that her mother had set, a standard she knew she'd never be able to achieve. Then she had a powerful insight, one that she would recount in O, The Oprah Magazine.

> *She was holding herself to a standard that her mother had set, a standard she knew she'd never be able to achieve.*

Shonda admired her mother for being a supermom and longed to be a mother too. So she contacted an adoption agency, filled out the necessary paperwork, and waited.

When a match was made, Shonda thought about the example her mother had set and panicked. "How am I going to be somebody's mother?" she asked herself.

Shonda phoned her mother, shared the news, and listed all the reasons she wasn't ready to raise a child. Her mother didn't say anything at first. Then she began to laugh. She assured her daughter that she didn't need to fret over the details, that love was the true measure of motherhood. Listening, really listening, to her mother's words sparked an epiphany for Shonda. It redefined what it meant to be a mom and gave her the confidence she needed.

For Jill Scott, it was an aunt's negative example that led to a momentous epiphany. When Jill was a girl, she had loved being with her aunt. Their time together overflowed with fun, laughter, and affection. Jill also witnessed the verbal abuse that her uncle heaped upon his wife. She would ask her aunt why she stayed in the relationship. The answer was always the same. Marriage is a lifetime commitment. Jill vowed that if she ever had the financial means she would help her aunt leave the marriage and construct a new life.

When Jill's singing career took off, she bought her aunt a house in the hope that she'd accept the assistance. Her aunt did but wasn't able to enjoy her new freedom for long. Within a year Jill's aunt was diagnosed with cancer. Chemotherapy and radiation treatments weren't enough to save her, and she died at the age of fifty-six.

When Jill lost her aunt, she experienced an insight that revealed the holes in her own marriage. After her epiphany, she found the courage to leave her husband, and find peace within herself.

For Chitra Banerjee Divakaruni, a disheartening shift in her mother's expectations triggered a life-changing realization. When she was little her mom had encouraged her to do well in school. But when Chitra was ten years old, she was devastated to discover the limits of her mother's support.

It was a summer day, and Chitra had just learned that she was no longer allowed to play with the neighborhood children, even though the same restriction didn't apply to her older brother. When Chitra questioned her mother about the disparity, she learned that standards were different for girls. She was shocked at this revelation, and disappointed in her mother.

Later that day, Chitra found the story of Sultana Raziyya in her brother's schoolbook. She was heartened by the example of the thirteenth century ruler of Delhi, a woman who had stood firm in the face of sexism. As Chitra read about Sultana Raziyya, she experienced an epiphany. It gave her the courage to remain true to herself despite limiting cultural expectations.

In the study, following the lead of a VIP was sometimes problematic, but in each case an epiphany put the person back on course.

▼ ▼ ▼

As for Angela Bassett, she reconsidered her course of study. With graduation just a year away, she wouldn't have time to earn a theater degree. She opted instead to change her major to African-American studies with a minor in theater.

Angela took as many drama courses as she could during her senior year at Yale. She wrote a performance thesis in addition to the one required for her major. She also applied to a graduate program at the Yale School of Drama and was accepted.

After earning her master of fine arts degree, Angela worked hard to establish her career. She eventually stepped into the spotlight, landing prominent roles on stage, on television, and in film. Over time, Angela became best known for her roles in biographical works, portraying Rosa Parks in *The Rosa Parks Story*, Betty Shabazz in *Malcolm X*, and Tina Turner in *What's Love Got to Do with It?*

▼ ▼ ▼

Following the lead of a VIP wasn't always a good idea. Even so, it could help set the stage for a powerful AHA!.

A NOTE TO YOU

Are there situations in which your VIPs are out of sync with who you are or who you want to become?

Your VIPs mean well. Yet the suggestions they give, the behaviors they expect, and the models they set might not work for you. Even then, if you notice the misalignment, you might spark an insight.

Beware of what's not a fit for you.

Trigger 4
Discover a new perspective in distressful situations

Alan Alda was desperate. An hour earlier he had heard a gurgle in his gut and felt a small cramp. Now the pain was so intense that he needed medical attention—and fast. But there was a problem. Alan had just finished filming at the Cerro Tololo Observatory in Chile. The closest hospital was in the small town of La Serena, an hour and a half away.

A surgeon was waiting at the hospital when the ambulance arrived. His diagnosis—a blocked intestine requiring immediate surgery. Then the surgeon explained the options. He could perform the procedure, or Alan could be flown to a larger hospital in Santiago. Unfortunately La Serena was fogged in, and the airport was closed. The fog might not dissipate in time.

Alan calmly opted to stay in La Serena. He thought about his wife and family and asked a friend to jot down a message in case he didn't survive. As Alan observed his own reaction to the situation, he experienced a flash of clarity. He suddenly saw that he need not fear death, and became fearless in life.

Experiencing desperate situations ignited life-changing realizations in thirteen percent of the accounts in the study. It involved being alert during harrowing moments. Trying times, though, weren't always enough to trigger a pivotal realization.

BE OBSERVANT DURING
LIFE'S HARROWING MOMENTS

Cory Booker saved a man's life, and in that instant he had a life-changing insight, one that put his priorities in order. It was a day that he would later describe in an interview with Susan Headden for *U.S. News & World Report.*

Cory had grown up in Harrington Park, New Jersey, an affluent neighborhood twenty miles northeast of Newark. His parents, Cary and Carolyn, worked for IBM. Both had risen to executive positions and were among the first African-American leaders in the company. Cory's parents were also active in the civil rights movement and would often take their children with them to rallies.

> *Cory Booker saved a man's life, and in that instant he had a life-changing insight.*

The Bookers found the house in Harrington Park around the time Cory was born. Unfortunately, the home was already sold—or so they were told. The Bookers contacted the New Jersey Fair Housing Commission, which sent a white couple to bid on the house on behalf of the Bookers. The second offer was accepted, and soon the Booker family had moved into the all-white neighborhood.

Years passed. Cory went to high school where he played football and served as the senior class president. He knew everyone—the teachers, the students, the staff. His outgoing personality earned him a nickname—the Mayor.

After graduating from high school, Cory attended Stanford University on a full football scholarship. He worked hard to keep his grades up, because he knew that his future lay in a graduate degree, not in professional sports. He also participated in student government and volunteered at The Bridge, a counseling hotline for the university and surrounding community.

In the fall of 1990, Cory began his senior year, and in October the football team traveled to South Bend, Indiana, to play Notre Dame. The Stanford team had little hope of winning. They weren't having a great season, they hadn't won a single away game in three years, and they were playing the best team in the country.

The starting whistle blew, and Notre Dame established a comfortable twenty-four to seven lead. Then Stanford began to close the gap—recovering fumbles, making touchdowns, and finally pulling ahead with only thirty-six seconds left in the game.

With six seconds on the game clock, the Notre Dame offense lined up for one last play. The quarterback took the snap and threw a pass into the end zone. The ball hit the receiver's hands, and dropped to the ground. Stanford had won! The final score was thirty-six to thirty-one.

Cory had played well in the game, with four catches that contributed to the win. Going pro was suddenly an option, and Cory started planning for a professional football career.

Later in the school year, Cory was on duty at The Bridge, and when the phone rang, he took the call. The man on the line was threatening suicide. He said that he was standing on the ledge of a building. He was going to jump.

Cory decided that it wouldn't work to counsel the caller through the phone line. Instead, he joined the man on the ledge. As they talked, Cory tried to convince him to give life a second chance. Minutes ticked by. Finally the man made his decision. He reached for Cory, the two hooked hands, and Cory pulled him to safety. Their touch sparked a momentous epiphany for Cory that showed him that he valued service over sports, and changed his choice of careers.

▼ ▼ ▼

Harrowing moments triggered pivotal realizations in thirteen percent of the accounts in the study. Cory, Alan Alda, and Trudie Styler, for example, faced life-threatening situations. Jill Scott and Bonnie Friedman experienced the death of loved ones, while Cynthia Nixon risked losing custody of her children. Iman and Mia Hamm suffered injuries that had the potential to end their careers.

Mia Hamm grew up playing soccer. It was her life. Then in 2002 she suffered a serious injury, but gained a life-changing insight.

Mia had joined the U.S. women's national soccer team in 1987. She was just fifteen years old—the team's youngest player ever. The squad notched a number of impressive wins over the next decade. In 1991 they defeated Norway to take the first ever Women's World Cup championship.

She suffered a serious injury, but gained a life-changing insight.

In 1996 women's soccer was added to the roster of events at the Summer Olympics, and the U.S. defeated China to earn a gold medal. In 1999 the American team reclaimed the World Cup title in another win over China. That same year Mia scored her 109th goal in international play—a record irrespective of gender.

The Women's United Soccer Association was formed in 2001. At twenty-nine, Mia finally had the opportunity to play professional sports. Then the unthinkable happened. Mia injured her knee during the 2002 preseason. She underwent surgery and endured months of rehabilitation while worrying about her career.

Mia returned to competition in June and scored her team's winning goal. As she sat in the locker room after the game, she was struck by an insight that dissolved her fears. Suddenly she saw that life would go on, with or without soccer.

Trudie Styler almost drowned in a Brazilian river, but emerged from the water having experienced a powerful AHA!.

Trudie had worked hard to build a successful acting career. When it stalled, she felt like a failure. She lost her confidence, and she began to believe she wasn't worthy of her family and her life.

Trudie and her partner Sting had founded the Rainforest Foundation. When the foundation's staff invited Trudie back to Brazil to see what they had been able to achieve, she hesitated but traveled with the foundation team deep into the rainforest. A group of young boys at one stop invited Trudie out onto the Xingu River.

> *Suddenly she saw that she had allowed others to determine her destiny.*

She opted in, piling with the boys into an undersized rowboat. They pulled hard on the oars as they made their way out to a sandbar in the middle of the river. On the return trip, the boys challenged each other to swim to shore, and several of them leapt into the water. Trudie jumped in too, and almost drowned.

As she struggled against the current, Trudie experienced a life-changing epiphany. Suddenly she saw that she had allowed others to determine her destiny. Once she had pulled herself from the river, she set about taking control of her life.

Experiencing harrowing situations sparked momentous epiphanies in several accounts in the study.

▼ ▼ ▼

As for Cory Booker, after his AHA! he stopped planning on a career in professional sports. He instead pursued a career in public service.

On graduation day, Cory received a bachelor's degree in political science. That fall he returned to Stanford to attend graduate school and earned a master's degree in sociology the following spring. After receiving a Rhodes scholarship, he left for England to study at Oxford University.

When Cory returned to the U.S., he enrolled in the Yale University School of Law. While still a law student, he began to focus on the city of Newark. He volunteered with children's programs, provided legal advice to residents of low-income housing, and moved into public housing himself in order to understand the lives of those he hoped to serve.

Fellow tenants urged Cory to run for a seat on Newark's City Council in 1998. He did and was elected. In 2002 Cory campaigned for the office of mayor, running against a long-time incumbent. Cory lost by a narrow margin, but in 2006 he ran again and won.

"I don't think there is anything more noble about my choice. We do what we know; we do what we love. And I love being in the thick of it," Cory told Headden as he reflected on his career in public service.

▼ ▼ ▼

Desperate situations can trigger life-changing epiphanies.

A NOTE TO YOU

Are you struggling with a matter of life-or-death, with the loss of a loved one, or with a threat to your family or to your career?

An insight might await you in your distress.

Be observant during life's harrowing moments.

DON'T TROUBLE TROUBLE

Bonnie Friedman had a philosophy for living. "Life is short and mustn't be wasted," she would tell herself. It sounded good, and she believed it. But for some reason she wasn't able to live life that way.

Bonnie thought about her life's philosophy after an acquaintance suffered a skydiving accident. When the woman's parachute malfunctioned, she plummeted thousands of feet. She landed in a field, survived, and went on to reinvent her life. While Bonnie wished that she could learn from her friend's experience, somehow she couldn't.

Another time, a car hit Bonnie as she walked along a street. Her body launched several feet into the air. While Bonnie would have liked to have learned from that horrifying experience too, somehow she couldn't.

When her older sister died, Bonnie had a pivotal insight and was finally able to put her philosophy into practice. She would recall that experience in an article for *O, The Oprah Magazine.*

As a child Bonnie had longed to be close to her mom—to touch her and cling to her. When her mother would lose patience and shoo her away, Bonnie would search out her sister, Anita, to fill the void. Bonnie would sit close to her sister and watch her as she worked.

> *When her older sister died, Bonnie had a pivotal insight.*

Anita was a master of so many things. She knew how to crayon bright colors onto a page, cover them with black, and then scratch exciting scenes with a pin. She knew how to cut sponges into shapes, soak them in paint, and create scenes perfect in their imperfection. She knew how to cut sheets of typing paper into rectangles, sew them into palm-sized books, and fill their pages with captivating stories.

Bonnie adored Anita. She marveled at her skills. She wanted to become just like her.

After Anita finished college, she spent some time in Israel. She returned home with a tingling sensation in her elbow that wouldn't go away. Eventually a diagnosis was made. Anita had multiple sclerosis.

Years passed while Anita stayed close to home and Bonnie moved away. Anita eventually married and so did Bonnie. As Anita's health declined Bonnie had to let go of her sister little by little.

When Anita died, Bonnie lit a mourning candle and placed it on her stove. After a week had passed, Bonnie blew out the flame and had an AHA! that gave her what she had desperately wanted to find.

▼ ▼ ▼

Does a life-threatening situation guarantee a life-changing epiphany? It didn't for Bonnie. She could have been seriously injured when she was struck by a car, and an acquaintance could have died when her parachute didn't deploy. Yet neither event was enough to convince Bonnie to change. Then Anita died, and Bonnie had a flash of clarity that changed the way she lived her life.

Life is precious and should be cherished. Bonnie was relieved to finally get the message. She immediately began to make adjustments in her life. She took greater care of her students, she made time to be with her parents, and she worked on her marriage.

▼ ▼ ▼

Distressing events don't always lead to transformational realizations.

A NOTE TO YOU

Are you hoping that a harrowing situation will trigger a pivotal epiphany for you? It might. And, it might not.

Desperate situations don't guarantee a momentous insight.

So, don't push your luck. Don't tempt fate. Don't trouble trouble.

Capture
the Value

▼ ▼ ▼

Certain actions helped people capitalize on their pivotal epiphanies. Once you've experienced your own powerful AHA!, you can take steps to boost its impact in your life. This section explains how.

▼ ▼ ▼

Clarify the message

For Nikki Giovanni being an author wasn't just about creating poetry. She savored writing in any form—minutes of meetings included. She enjoyed sharing her craft—regardless of the audience. And she knew the importance of looking at the world through a writer's eyes—even when she forgot to do so herself.

Nikki had joined the English department at Virginia Tech in 1987. Soon afterward she began volunteering at the Warm Hearth retirement home. Whether working with college students or with retirees, Nikki believed that everyone could write, and she relished teaching people how.

Nikki would give her students writing advice. Don't ignore your natural rhythms. Write in your own voice. Don't layer outside influences onto your work. Concentrate on telling the story. Don't worry about the length of what you write. Focus on adding information. Mostly though, Nikki would help her students see the stories in the world around them—to look at the sum, the parts, and the nuance.

Nikki spent her days writing, teaching, and speaking, and as the years rolled by, she overlooked a central element of her own life. Then Nikki experienced a powerful insight as she drove to visit a friend in another state. She would later describe the AHA!

in an article for *O, The Oprah Magazine.*

The day of the road trip had arrived. Nikki and a friend piled into Nikki's little red sports car and zipped along the highway toward Princeton, New Jersey. They were feeling young and hip. It didn't matter that Nikki was pushing the age of sixty. She still considered herself a babe.

By midnight Nikki and her friend were lost and tired. Then Nikki caught the unwelcome sight of a state trooper behind her. She pulled over, rolled down her window, and waited. She knew she was going to get a ticket.

"You were drifting across the center line," the young patrolman told her as he leaned down and shone his flashlight into the car. As the beam of light swept across Nikki's face, he suddenly stepped back. His tone changed and he addressed Nikki as "ma'am." He didn't write Nikki a ticket. He didn't even want to see her driver's license. Instead, he gave the women directions, suggested they stop for coffee, and cautioned them to drive safely.

The interaction with the trooper sparked an insight for Nikki. "We're *old*!" she exclaimed and then said to her friend, "You drive—I need to think about what just happened."

▼ ▼ ▼

In the study, an insight's implications were usually clear right away. For example when Bette Midler discovered a Manhattan park piled with trash two stories high, she had a powerful AHA! and knew at once that she needed to redouble her efforts to clean up the city.

Christine Ebersole was forty-five when she noticed the negative reactions of others in Hollywood to her age and realized that she was considered past her professional prime. Instantly she knew that she needed to get back on stage in New York City. There she would be judged by her capabilities, not by her age.

And when Dorothy Allison witnessed her mother's capacity to laugh in the face of hardship, she had an epiphany. In a flash of understanding she saw the importance of standing in joy in the midst of life's difficulties.

While the implications of a pivotal realization were obvious in the majority of cases, it took additional time to clarify the meaning of an insight in seven percent of the accounts in the study. That was true for Nikki, Sandra Oh, Hillary Rodham Clinton, and Harry Connick Jr., among others.

> *In a flash of understanding she saw the importance of standing in joy in the midst of life's difficulties.*

After Sandra Oh was struck by an AHA!, she needed time to figure out what it meant to her life's work. She had hit it lucky early in her career by starring in three Canadian films. Her Korean heritage had made her a perfect fit for the roles.

When Sandra moved to Los Angeles, she knew she'd face rejection at times—especially as a minority actor. But when a white friend was granted an audition and she wasn't, she suddenly realized just how high the hurdles would be. She stopped to weigh the implications of the insight to her career, and eventually opted to persist as an actor.

When Hillary Rodham Clinton experienced a powerful insight, she paused to consider its impact on a decision she was trying to make. She had been thinking about running for the U.S. Senate, but she couldn't decide. She wavered even after consulting with a number of knowledgeable and influential people. It was the comment of a teenager that triggered an epiphany for Hillary.

In a moment of clarity she recognized that she wasn't following her own advice, advice she had given other women.

That night Hillary couldn't sleep. She replayed the exchange with the teenager over and over in her mind and examined her reluctance to run for the Senate seat. Morning came. Hillary was still thinking about the insight. Before long she made the decision to launch her campaign.

After an AHA! hit Harry Connick Jr., he reconsidered his approach to raising his children. Earlier on the day of his insight, Harry had steered his two-year-old daughter out the door of their house. They were headed to the park but progress was slow. The toddler was more interested in the pebbles in the driveway than she was in getting to the park.

Harry noticed his impatience and had a pivotal realization. He slowed down to rethink his approach to parenting, opted to become a different kind of father, and devoted quite a bit of time that day to exploring the world of rocks.

After experiencing an epiphany, some individuals in the study needed time to clarify the meaning of the message.

▼ ▼ ▼

As for Nikki, her insight led her to embrace her age. She joined AARP and started taking better care of herself. She also allowed herself to have more fun with her writing and to enjoy the creative process.

▼ ▼ ▼

The meaning of an epiphany is often obvious, but sometimes it's not.

A NOTE TO YOU

You've experienced a flash of clarity. Congratulations!

What's your insight telling you? The message could be clear. Or, it could be confusing, unsettling, or uncertain.

If you're not sure about the meaning of your AHA!, take time to think about it and to clarify the message.

Try it on to make sure it fits

Maria Shriver faced a dilemma. She didn't know what she wanted to be when she grew up—despite already being a journalist, a mother, an author, a member of the Kennedy clan, and the First Lady of California. Then her teenage daughter informed her that the time to decide had already passed. Maria worried that her daughter might be right.

Maria had been a teenager herself when she discovered journalism. The year was 1972. George McGovern had just won the Democratic nomination for president. Sargent Shriver, Maria's father, was McGovern's running mate.

Maria traveled with her father as he campaigned. She sat in the rear of the plane with the journalists, and was hooked. After college she focused on building her career. She loved journalism and couldn't imagine doing anything else. Eventually she became an anchorwoman for NBC News.

When her husband, Arnold Schwarzenegger, ran for governor of California and won, the executives at NBC News recognized the potential for a perceived conflict of interest. They thought it would be best if Maria resigned. She did. But after she had left her job, she found she had lost her sense of self.

One day Maria's nephew called to ask her to speak at his high school graduation. The timing couldn't have been worse. Maria didn't have answers for her own future, much less for others. So she declined. But when her nephew persisted, she eventually said yes. The experience that followed would lead to insights so significant that Maria would write about them in a book titled *Just Who Will You Be?*

After she had left her job, she found she had lost her sense of self.

Maria agonized over what to tell the graduates. She rewrote her speech several times. For the life of her she couldn't figure out what they wanted her to say.

By graduation day, Maria had written *Just Who Will You Be?*, a poem in which she urged the graduates to be guided by their hearts, their passions, and their dreams—not by the expectations of others.

After the speech Maria described the experience to a friend, recounting the ordeal and her message. Their conversation sparked an insight for her. Suddenly and clearly she saw that she hadn't heeded her own advice. "Who will I be?" she began to ask herself.

As Maria contemplated the question, another epiphany struck. The second AHA! showed Maria *exactly* what she needed to do. She needed to convince NBC to ask her back! She made the pitch and NBC agreed. Maria was thrilled and made plans to return to work after Arnold's re-election campaign.

When Arnold won, Maria spoke at his inauguration. She recited a Hopi prayer. "This IS the Hour. Where are you living? What are you doing? What are your relations?" Then she reached the powerful final line of the poem. "It is time to speak your truth."

As days passed, the prayer stuck with Maria. The questions rattled around in her mind, and she was no longer sure about returning to NBC. So she decided to do something she had never done before. She went away by herself for a couple of days. The retreat was out of character for her. In fact, it was scary. But she went anyway.

She meditated. Sit, think, ask. Inhale. Exhale. Her questions were answered with more questions.

After returning home, Maria noticed something as she watched various newscasts. Things had changed since she left her job. The stories were different, and so was she. So Maria contacted NBC News to tell them that she wouldn't be returning.

Achieve in a big way. That's what a Kennedy would do, and that's what Maria had done—until now. Pushing hard had once energized her, but those days were gone. Maria noticed the shift and had a third insight that helped her further hone her self-exploration. "Who will I be?" was no longer the question. Instead Maria began to ask, "Just who *do* I want to be?"

▼ ▼ ▼

How often does a person write about an insight that fizzled? Maria did. An epiphany had convinced her she needed to decide who she would be. A second AHA! pointed her back to her former job at NBC, but she quickly discovered that the second realization didn't fit the person she had become.

The first insight fit. The second one didn't. It took recognizing the mismatch to spark a third epiphany for Maria, one that helped her along the path of self-discovery.

▼ ▼ ▼

"Just who *do* I want I be?" Maria continued her search despite the trepidation she felt. As she drew closer to an answer, she got to know herself better, and she learned a number of valuable lessons. "But most important," she wrote, "I will try to live an authentic life that feels true to me—which means living life as myself, not an imitation of anyone else, and not the reflection of myself in anyone else's eyes."

▼ ▼ ▼

An epiphany can arrive with a jolt and a flourish and yet be out of sync with who a person is and who she hopes to become.

A NOTE TO YOU

Take some time to live with your new insight.

Does it fit who you are and what you believe? Does it put you in a better position to achieve your goals and to live your values?

It might. And, it might not.

Try it on to make sure it fits.

Get to work

Norman Vincent Peale grew up in southern Ohio during the early years of the twentieth century. He dreamed of being a public speaker. He would picture himself standing before large audiences. He would visualize himself speaking with eloquence, and the people would be moved. Sadly Norman knew he would never achieve his goal.

He had plenty of role models. His father, a Methodist minister, spoke with power, persuasion, and assurance. His mother, a storyteller, stirred listeners to laughter and to tears. And his Uncle Will, a salesman, painted verbal pictures so vivid they enticed even the most wary buyers.

Inadequate. That's how Norman felt. He lacked ability, he lacked intelligence, and he was sure he would be a failure.

Each September Norman's father attended the Methodist district conference. The district superintendent always announced pastoral appointments at the close of the meeting. Reassigned ministers would pull their children out of school, pack their belongings, and transport their families to new parsonages.

As a minister's son, Norman lived in more than a dozen houses while he was growing up. The frequent moves increased the bond he felt with his family, but did little for his self-confidence.

In 1916 Norman enrolled at Ohio Wesleyan University. While a student there, he experienced an insight so momentous that he would write about it in the preface of one of the many editions of his seminal book, *The Power of Positive Thinking*.

At college, Norman joined the Phi Delta Gamma fraternity and moved into the fraternity house. He settled in easily, enjoying the camaraderie of his fraternity brothers, but self-doubt followed Norman into the classroom.

Most of the courses at Ohio Wesleyan combined lectures by professors with recitations by students. Norman knew the material well, but when he was called on to recite, he would be overcome by anxiety. His face would flush, he would stumble over his words, and his fellow students would snicker.

One day a professor asked Norman to stay after class. He spoke sternly and directly to the young man and described what he had observed—both the self-doubt *and* the capabilities. He told Norman it was time to give up his insecurities.

Norman staggered from the room, out the building, and down the steps. Tears filled his eyes as he simultaneously fumed and despaired.

"Then I stopped short," Norman wrote. "I recall the exact spot—the fourth step from the bottom—for a thought had pierced my mind. It was the exciting, almost incredible thought, 'I don't need to be this way any longer!'"

Norman stayed where he stood while he said a prayer, and then he stepped into a new life. Certain that he needed to change his thinking, but not knowing how, he searched for guidance and discovered the writings of William James, Ralph Waldo Emerson, Marcus Aurelius, and others. Little by little Norman changed his thinking, and his life.

▼ ▼ ▼

A flash of clarity pointed Norman toward a new life, *and* it gave him the confidence, the resolve, and the dedication to get there. All he had to do was to supply the effort.

Norman was not alone. In forty-one percent of the cases in the study, it took considerable work to follow through on a pivotal realization. That held true for Cecelia Rosenberg Daniels, Josh Hamilton, and Glenn Close, among others.

> *A flash of clarity pointed Norman toward a new life.*

Cecelia Rosenberg Daniels had a life-changing insight that sent her back to school. She had started her career as a social worker but stopped working to be a stay-at-home mom. The decades slipped by, her children grew up, and Cecelia pushed past the fifty-year mark.

Then the unthinkable happened—her darling cat disappeared, and Cecelia was crushed. She noticed her reaction to the loss and experienced a transformational AHA!. In a flash of clarity, she saw that there were weightier issues in the world than a missing cat. With a broadened perspective, Cecelia decided to return to school, and at the age of fifty-nine, she became an attorney practicing family law.

Josh Hamilton experienced an epiphany that empowered him to overcome a drug addiction.

Josh loved baseball. It was his life. In 1999 he had been the Major League's number one draft pick, signing with the Tampa Bay Devil Rays. Then in 2001 Josh injured his shoulder in a traffic accident, and the Devil Rays had to play without him.

Josh wrestled with boredom and began to experiment with drugs. It didn't take long for cocaine to become his life. He lost his career, his family, and his health. Then a pivotal realization showed him how his decision to do drugs had closed him off from everything that was important. Josh was then able to began piecing his life back together, one step at a time.

Glenn Close had a flash of clarity that required her to become comfortable speaking about mental health issues.

She had not recognized the signs of mental illness in her family. Not when her grandmother took periodic trips to a place called Silver Hill. Not when her younger sister grappled with drug overdoses, troubled relationships, and unstable moods. Not even when she prepared herself to play the role of troubled Alex Forrest in the movie *Fatal Attraction*.

When Glenn's nephew was diagnosed with schizo-affective disorder and his mother—her sister—was diagnosed as bipolar, Glenn finally recognized the pattern of mental illness in her family. But seeing it and being able to talk about it were two different things. As she noticed her fear and shame, she experienced a powerful epiphany. Suddenly she knew that she needed to move past the stigma and to help others do the same. So Glenn got to work, first becoming comfortable discussing mental health issues, and then encouraging others to join the dialogue.

In many of the cases in the study, the experience of an epiphany wasn't the end of the story. It was, instead, the beginning of a lot of work.

As for Norman Vincent Peale, after his insight he eventually created a new way of thinking for himself and began to share it with others. He preached about it in his sermons. He wrote about it in a weekly newspaper column that reached ten million readers, and he spoke about it in a weekly radio broadcast that reached three million listeners. He also co-founded *Guideposts* magazine and wrote more than forty books, one of which, *The Power of Positive Thinking*, became one of the most successful nonfiction books of all time.

A life-changing insight will point toward a new destination, but it won't supply the effort needed to get there.

A NOTE TO YOU

A flash of clarity has put you on a new path and has given you the energy, the motivation, and the resolve to change.

What will it take to follow through on your AHA!? Considerable effort might be required.

If so, get to work.

Go for gold!

Karen Barber had her workday routines. Monday through Thursday, she would begin her day at 6:00 a.m. with a morning walk. Then she would sit down to write. At breaks during the day, she would scan the newspaper for garage sales, her Friday custom. Little did Karen know that in the routines of her day she would find insights so compelling that she would write about them for *Guideposts* magazine.

It was a Friday morning, garage-sale day. Karen had stuffed her fanny pack with small bills, fastened it around her waist, and headed out ready to bargain.

A lamp at one stop caught Karen's eye. Sure it needed a new shade, but it was one of a kind—maybe even an antique. It was priced at ten dollars, but Karen offered eight. When the seller readily accepted the lower price, Karen was annoyed. She told herself that she should have offered even less.

Karen lugged the lamp home only to find that it didn't match her décor. So she decided to put it in her office. Her husband would be less likely to see it there. What *he* didn't notice, *she* didn't have to explain.

Karen set the lamp on the desk and plugged it in, but it didn't light. A new bulb made no difference. As she hauled the lamp to the basement, she scolded herself for not asking the seller whether it worked.

On Monday morning, Karen finished her walk and sat down at her desk. She tried to write but couldn't find her focus. Her thoughts kept drifting back to the lamp. Why did she buy it in the first place? Is a bargain really a bargain if it's broken? As Karen thought about her drive to buy things she didn't need, she spotted her Bible lying nearby and glanced at the open page. As she read that life is more than possessions, Karen suddenly saw the source of her problem and knew she had to change her approach to bargain hunting.

That AHA! cooled Karen's garage-sale fever, but it wasn't the only flash of clarity that she would experience. She had another insight that solved a health dilemma. When Karen had turned fifty-four, her doctor recommended a bone scan, a routine procedure for someone her age. Karen had the test and forgot about it until a nurse from her HMO called to tell her that she would be receiving a prescription for osteoporosis medication. The nurse explained how to take the pills and then asked if she had any questions. Dumbfounded, Karen said no.

Osteoporosis? Karen couldn't believe it. She was young, and healthy. Besides, she took good care of herself.

In the days and weeks that followed, Karen found reasons to avoid taking the medication. She was going on vacation. She needed to talk to the doctor to make sure there wasn't a mistake. She was too busy to risk the side effects.

On a weekday morning, Karen headed out the door for her morning walk, praying as she went. She walked through her backyard, across the creek, and up the hill to a road where she began a prayer of thanksgiving. She had so many things to be grateful for—her husband, her sons, the lovely spring morning, the pills. "The pills?" Karen asked herself with a start, and in that moment she saw the medication in a new light.

▼ ▼ ▼

Karen had a powerful AHA! that changed her approach to bargain hunting. She also had a momentous insight that altered her view of the medication that her physician had prescribed. She was not alone. Eight percent of the individuals in the study described more than one life-altering epiphany. (The actual percentage is likely higher, and possibly much higher, since the research was not focused on determining the number of pivotal realizations each individual had experienced.)

Two accounts of life-changing epiphanies were identified for six individuals—Karen, Phil Keoghan, Maria Shriver, Bernie Mac, Marcia Gay Harden, and Maria Bello. Three accounts were identified for Angela Bassett.

Bernie Mac experienced a powerful insight when he was a young boy, and he was struck by another AHA! when he was in his early twenties.

Bernie was just five years old when an epiphany showed him the transforming effect of laughter. He had noticed that his mother was crying and crawled onto her lap to hold her hand and wipe away her tears. Bernie asked his mom what was wrong, but she wouldn't tell him. No one knew that she was battling breast cancer, and she certainly wasn't going to burden her little boy with the news.

> *An epiphany showed him the transforming effect of laughter.*

The television in their apartment was tuned to the *Ed Sullivan Show*, and that night Bill Cosby was a featured guest. Bernie and his mom, who was still crying, watched as Bill wove a funny, funny tale. Bernie noticed that his mom began to chuckle and then to laugh. He laughed too.

As Bernie saw the shift in his mother's mood, he experienced an insight. It showed him the power of humor and set him on a path to becoming a comedian.

Bernie was a teenager when his mother died of cancer. He married at nineteen and was a father by twenty. As Bernie struggled to provide for his family, he considered giving up comedy, something he loved. Then the words of his mother came to mind, words that encouraged him to give his all in every situation. In a flash of clarity, Bernie recognized that abandoning comedy wouldn't be right. He simply needed to do his best for himself and for his audiences.

Maria Bello was hit by an insight when she was an undergraduate student. Years later she experienced a second insight as she thought about the first. She had been a freshman in college when she met Father Ray Jackson, a professor who became her mentor. Father Ray encouraged Maria to focus her career on what she loved. His advice sparked an epiphany for Maria, one that gave her the nudge she needed to pursue an acting career.

Years later Maria sat down to write about the epiphany for *O, The Oprah Magazine*. As she thought about Father Ray, who had died soon after she graduated, she experienced another pivotal insight. Devotion to the people she loved, she realized, was the greatest gift she could ever give. In the days that followed, she focused on demonstrating her new understanding.

In the study, several people reported more than one life-changing insight, and as a result, experienced even greater benefits in their lives.

▼ ▼ ▼

As for Karen Barber, did she give up garage sales? Absolutely not. She continued her Friday tradition, but with one important change. She created a list of bargain-hunting rules and bought only items that fit the new criteria.

And what about the osteoporosis medication? After the insight Karen began to take her pills, and was grateful to have them.

▼ ▼ ▼

A person isn't limited to one pivotal epiphany over the course of a lifetime.

A NOTE TO YOU

Why stop with one insight? Imagine the impact on your life of having two, three, or thirty of them.

Set your sights high. Go for gold!

Pull It All Together

▼ ▼ ▼

Prime yourself. Watch for triggers. Capture the value. Those three sections showed you how to prepare yourself for a life-changing insight. Now, it's time to pull it all together. Whether you've already experienced an AHA! or are still waiting, remember to practice both patience and impatience.

▼ ▼ ▼

Practice patience
and impatience

Ron Blomberg grew up in Atlanta. Baseball was his life—and so was impatience. He knew he couldn't wait around if he was going to make it to the majors, and then he had an insight that changed his perspective. It was an experience so moving that he would write about it in an article for *Guideposts* magazine.

When he was an eight-year-old boy, Ron had stood in line at Little League tryouts waiting for his number to be called. He showed the coaches what he could do but didn't make the cut. Instead of going home, he took another number, tried again, and made the team.

Ron was a natural athlete. By the time he was nine, he had earned a place on a team of twelve-year-olds, and by his freshman year in high school, he had caught the attention of a Major League scout. In high school he lettered in four sports—baseball, basketball, football, and track.

It was a spring day, and the high school baseball team was hard at practice. Ron wanted to work on his swing. He stood in line for the batting cage, but the guys ahead of him were too slow. Unable to wait, Ron cut in front of his teammates. The coach saw what

Ron had done and reminded him of the importance of patience. Ron laughed and told the coach he didn't have time to stand around.

Ron signed with the New York Yankees, his favorite team, the day after his high school graduation in 1967. After the fanfare of signing, Ron was sent to a minor league team. He would have to earn his way to Yankee Stadium.

Four seasons came and went, and Ron still hadn't made it to the majors. He had made good progress, but he didn't see it. He was tired of waiting.

In 1971 Ron joined the Yankees at spring training camp. He had been there before but had always been sent back to the minors. He was determined that this year would be different, so he pushed himself hard, too hard. It affected his performance at bat and in the outfield. Then one day as Ron scrambled to snag a fly ball, he hurt his back.

That spring, Ron was among the first players booted back to the minors. He fumed as he packed his bags. He'd had enough. He was done. Instead of accepting the assignment, he went home.

After temple one evening, Ron described his ordeal and his decision to quit baseball to his rabbi. When the rabbi asked Ron what he was passionate about, Ron didn't hesitate. Baseball. The rabbi advised him to slow down and give God time. Ron said that he was through with waiting.

He was struck by an epiphany, suddenly seeing the down side of his impatience.

A few days later Ron made plans to catch a movie with his wife, Mara. He was ready to go, but she was still getting dressed. Impatient, Ron shouted for her to hurry up.

Mara emerged from the bedroom wearing an angry look.

"Can't you wait for anything?" she snapped.

Her anger caught Ron off guard. As he apologized, he was struck by an epiphany, suddenly seeing the down side of his impatience.

▼ ▼ ▼

Unwillingness to wait worked for Ron, but it also got in his way. And while the benefits of impatience were immediately clear to him, it took time for him to discover the down side.

Ron had to wait for his insight, and he was not alone. A delay to some extent was a factor in sixty-nine percent of the cases in the study including those of Annie Lennox and Isabella Rossellini, among others.

Annie Lennox was almost fifty when a flash of clarity gave her insight into something that had long bothered her. She had always been troubled by the inequality she saw in the world. She knew there wasn't much that one person could do, so she did what she could but didn't get overly involved. Meanwhile, as the decades rolled by, she focused on building her singing career.

Then in 2003 Annie accepted an invitation from Nelson Mandela to participate in a charity concert in South Africa. After the performance, she attended a press conference and listened as Mr. Mandela described the devastating impact of HIV and AIDS on the people of Africa. In that moment Annie felt a connection with the women who were suffering and experienced a life-changing insight. It convinced her to get involved and led her to become an activist.

Isabella Rossellini had built two successful careers by the time she had an insight that suddenly showed her the wisdom of her parents' advice. When she was growing up, Isabella had often heard her parents say that she should follow her passion, for there she'd likely find her talents. She loved animals and enjoyed making films about them. But it was just frivolous fun, not something to build a career around. Instead she focused on succeeding as a model, actress, and mother.

Life changed for Isabella around the time she reached her mid-fifties. Her children didn't need her like they once did, she no longer modeled, and she acted in fewer roles. It would be a good time to return to school, she decided. Along the way she had a pivotal epiphany that finally gave her the freedom to follow her heart, and she began once again to focus on filming animals.

Waiting for an insight was required in many accounts in the study.

▼ ▼ ▼

I have found that impatience and patience are both important when generating life-changing realizations. My colleagues and I encourage our coaching clients to be impatient—to set their goals high, to push themselves, and to expect spectacular results. We also encourage them to be patient—to prime themselves for insight and then to wait with trust and confidence. That approach has worked well for our clients. Most of them

> *Impatience **and** patience are both important when generating life-changing realizations.*

have been able to generate transforming insights within a few months, often pushing past personal ceilings that had been in place for many years.

My hope for you is that you will experience the same profound impact in your life. And as you practice both patience and impatience, I'd love to know how things are going. What powerful AHA!s have you been able to generate? I can't wait to hear your stories. And are there places in your life where you continue to struggle? Perhaps I can give you some tips and point you toward resources. You can reach me through my website www.donnahartney.com.

▼ ▼ ▼

As for Ron Blomberg, he and Mara didn't go to the theater that night. Instead Ron dialed the Yankees' number, hoping that it wasn't too late.

Ron reported to the Yankees' farm team in Syracuse, New York. There he focused on being patient. That June he was called up to the majors where he had a great season, in addition to having learned an important life lesson.

▼ ▼ ▼

Transformational insights often take time. Yet, they can be coaxed along.

A NOTE TO YOU

Would you like to experience a life-changing flash of clarity?

If so, set your sights high, expect a breakthrough, and practice the epiphany-encouraging actions described in this book. Then wait, trusting that an insight will come.

Remember, practice both patience and impatience.

Study Sample

Agassi, Andre

Agassi, A. (2009). *Open: An autobiography*. New York: Alfred A. Knopf.

Andre Agassi biography. (n.d.). *bio.* Retrieved from http://www.biography.com

Finn, R. (1995, March 27). TENNIS; Agassi emerges triumphant this time by turning the tables on Sampras. *The New York Times.* Retrieved from http://www.nytimes.com/

Perrotta, T. (2010, August 13). The state of Roger Federer's skeleton: After a break, the 29-year-old returns to defy the laws of tennis decay; those vulnerable hips. *The Wall Street Journal.* Retrieved from http://professional.wsj.com/article/SB10001424052748704388504575419440012876632.html?mg=reno64-wsj

Alda, Alan

Alan Alda's aha! moment: The big change. (2006, March). *O, The Oprah Magazine, 7*(3). Retrieved from http://www.oprah.com/omagazine.html

Alan Alda goes "On the Record". (2005, November 30). *Fox News.com.* Retrieved from http://www.foxnews.com/

Alda, A. (2005). *Never Have Your Dog Stuffed: And other things I've learned*. New York: Random House.

Allison, Dorothy

Dorothy Allison's aha! moment. (2002, November). *O, The Oprah Magazine, 3*(11). Retrieved from http://www.oprah.com/omagazine.html

Apple, Fiona

Fiona Apple. (n.d.). *Rolling Stone.* Retrieved from http://www.rollingstone.com/music/artists/fiona-apple

Fiona Apple's aha! moment: Being wanted. (2006, March). *O, The Oprah Magazine, 7*(3). Retrieved from http://www.oprah.com/omagazine.html

Eliscu, J. (2005, October 6). Fiona Apple. *Rolling Stone, 984,* 64-66.

Loyal fans helped free Fiona Apple's CD: The troubled CD got mysteriously leaked onto the internet before release. (2005, October 5). *Today.com.* Retrieved from http://today.msnbc.msn.com/

Pareles, J. (2005, April 3). The lost apple. *The New York Times.* Retrieved from http://www.nytimes.com/

Scaggs, A. (2005, December 29). Fiona Apple. *Rolling Stone, 990/991,* 78-79.

Valby, K. (2005, September 30). The extraordinary truth. *Entertainment Weekly, 842,* 28-33.

Ball, Lucille

Ball, L. (1996). *Love, Lucy.* New York: G. P. Putnam's Sons.

Higham, C. (1986). *Lucy: The real life of Lucille Ball.* New York: St. Martin's Press.

Banerjee Divakaruni, Chitra (See Divakaruni, Chitra Banerjee)

Barber, Karen (2 insights)

Barber, K. (n.d.). Accepting osteoporosis: Finally recognizing the problem was a step forward in her self-improvement. *Guideposts.* Retrieved from http://www.guideposts.org (Original work published March 2009: "I'm too young for this". *Guideposts, 64*(1), 64-67.)

Barber, K. (n.d.). Junk junkie. In *Paths to Happiness: 7 real life stories of personal growth, self-improvement and positive change* (pp. 9-10). Retrieved from http://www.guideposts.org (Original work published May 2008: *Guideposts, 63*(3), 48-51.)

Bassett, Angela (3 insights)

Barr, N. (as told to). (2008, September). Angela Bassett's aha! moment. *O, The Oprah Magazine, 9*(9). Retrieved from http://www.oprah.com/omagazine.html

Bassett, A., & Vance, C. B. (with Beard, H.). (2007). *Friends: A love story.* New York: Kimani Press.

Bello, Maria (2 insights)

Maria Bello's aha! moment. (2006, February). *O, The Oprah Magazine, 7*(2). Retrieved from http://www.oprah.com/omagazine.html

Berry, Halle

Aha! moments. (2006, March). *O, The Oprah Magazine, 7*(3). Retrieved from http://www.oprah.com/omagazine.html

Halle Berry charged with misdemeanor in hit and run case. (2000, April 17). *Jet, 97*(19), 12.

Saying she doesn't recall incident, Halle Berry gets probation in hit and run case. (2000, May 29). *Jet, 97*(25), 36-37.

Blomberg, Ron

Blomberg, R. (n.d.). The power of patience. *Guideposts.* Retrieved from http://www.guideposts.org (Original work published August 1972: My waiting game. *Guideposts.*)

Blomberg, R., & Schlossberg, D. (2006). *Designated Hebrew: The Ron Blomberg story.* Champaign, IL: Sports Publishing.

Booker, Cory

1990 Notre Dame vs. Stanford [video]. (n.d.). *YouTube.* Retrieved from http://www.youtube.com/

Cory Booker. (2007, February). *Current Biography, 68*(2), 25-32.

Crowe, J. (1990, October 12). Upset of Notre Dame a study in restraint: Stanford: The band (of course) went wild after big victory, but many had other things to do. *Los Angeles Times.* Retrieved from http://articles.latimes.com/1990-10-12/sports/sp-2294_1_notre-dame

Headden, S. (2006, April 16). The guy in the thick of it. *U.S. News & World Report, 140*(15), 35-36, 38. Retrieved from http://www.usnews.com/usnews/biztech/articles/060424/24booker.htm

Stanford 2010 Football Media Guide. (2010). Retrieved from http://www.gostanford.com/media-guides/

The Bridge: 24/7 peer counseling and support. (n.d.). *Stanford University.* Retrieved from www.stanford.edu/group/bridge/Bridge/Welcome.html

Three Stanford students named Rhodes scholars for 1992. (1991, December 9). *Stanford University.* Retrieved from http://news.stanford.edu/pr/

Bowyer, Carmindy

Carmindy. (n.d.). Carmindy's inspiring life: A well-known makeup artist shares her story of overcoming a difficult childhood and discovering real beauty. *Guideposts.* Retrieved from http://www.guideposts.org (Original work published April 2010: A beautiful moment. *Guideposts, 65*(2), 32-36.)

Carmindy Bowyer: Celebrity. (n.d.). *TV Guide.* Retrieved from http://www.tvguide.com/

Buckley, Gail

Buckley, G. L. (1986). *The Hornes: An American family.* New York: Alfred A. Knopf.

Gail Buckley's aha! moment. (2001, August). *O, The Oprah Magazine, 2*(8). Retrieved from http://www.oprah.com/omagazine.html

Butler, Octavia

Elliott, D. (Host), & Ball, S. (Reporter). (2006, May 4). Octavia Butler: Eye on the stars, feet on the ground [Radio broadcast]. In *All Things Considered.* Retrieved from http://www.npr.org/

Francis, C. (Ed.). (2010). *Conversations with Octavia Butler.* Jackson: University Press of Mississippi.

Octavia Butler's aha! moment: Eye witness. (2002, May). *O, The Oprah Magazine, 3*(5). Retrieved from http://www.oprah.com/omagazine.html

Cardoso, Patricia

Patricia Cardoso's aha! moment. (2003, August). *O, The Oprah Magazine, 4*(8). Retrieved from http://www.oprah.com/omagazine.html

Carmindy (See Bowyer, Carmindy)

Carroll, Lenedra

Carroll, L. J. (2001). *The Architect of All Abundance: Creating a successful life in the material world.* Novato, CA: New World Library.

Lenedra Carroll's aha! moment. (2001, October). *O, The Oprah Magazine, 2*(10). Retrieved from http://www.oprah.com/omagazine.html

Chevalier, Tracy

Tracy Chevalier: About. (n.d.). Retrieved from http://www.tchevalier.com/

Tracy Chevalier's aha! moment. (2001, November). *O, The Oprah Magazine, 2*(11). Retrieved from http://www.oprah.com/omagazine.html

Clinton, Hillary Rodham

Aha! moments. (2006, March). *O, The Oprah Magazine, 7*(3). Retrieved from http://www.oprah.com/omagazine.html

Clinton, H. R. (2003). *Living History.* New York: Simon & Schuster.

Yates, M. (2004, December 31). She dared Senator Clinton to run, urges others to fight for their dreams. *The New York Sun.* Retrieved from http://www.nysun.com/

Close, Glenn

Close, G. (2010, September). No more secrets: We knew something was wrong in our family, but we never talked about it. *Guideposts, 65*(7), 50-54.

Schneller, J. (as told to). (2010, January). Glenn Close's aha! moment. *O, The Oprah Magazine, 11*(1). Retrieved from http://www.oprah.com/omagazine.html

Connick, Harry, Jr.

Harry Connick Jr.'s aha! moment. (2004, January). *O, The Oprah Magazine, 5*(1). Retrieved from http://www.oprah.com/omagazine.html

Cornelius, Bil

Cornelius, B. (2010). *I Dare You to Change!: Discover the difference between dreaming of a better life and living it.* New York: Guideposts.

Cornelius, B. (2010, October). Make your dreams come true: Never underestimate what you can achieve. *Guideposts, 65*(8), 56-59.

Curry, Ann

Curry, A. (2010, March). An act of faith. *Guideposts, 65*(1), 42-46.

Curry, Ann. (2004). In C. Thompson (Ed.), *Current Biography Yearbook: 65th annual cumulation* (pp. 107-109). New York: H. W. Wilson Company.

NBC journalist Ann Curry addresses the Class of 2010 [speech transcription]. (2010). *Wheaton College.* Retrieved from http://wheatoncollege.edu/

Daniels, Cecelia Rosenberg (See Rosenberg Daniels, Cecelia)

Davis, Hope

van der Leun, J. (as told to). (2007, August). Hope Davis' aha! moment. *O, The Oprah Magazine, 8*(8). Retrieved from http://www.oprah.com/omagazine.html

Delany, Dana

Bertsche, R. (as told to). (2008, October). Dana Delany's aha! moment. *O, The Oprah Magazine, 9*(10). Retrieved from http://www.oprah.com/omagazine.html

DiSpirito, Rocco

DiSpirito, R. (n.d.). Rocco DiSpirito's tasty success: He shares his inspiring story of how his mother helped him find his way. Retrieved from http://www.guideposts.org (Original work published May 2009: "Mama knew best". *Guide-posts, 64*(3), 30-33.)

Divakaruni, Chitra Banerjee

Chitra Banerjee Divakaruni: Background. (n.d.). Retrieved from http://www.chitradivakaruni.com

Chitra Divakaruni's aha! moment: "But you're a girl!". (2001, December). *O, The Oprah Magazine, 2*(12). Retrieved from http://www.oprah.com/omagazine.html

Davis, R. G. (2003). Chitra Banerjee Divakaruni. In G. Huang (Ed.), *Asian American Short Story Writers: An a-z guide* (pp. 65-67). Westport, CT: Greenwood Press.

Reese, L. (1995). Sultana Razia. In R. Ashby & D. G. Ohrn (Eds.), *Herstory: Women who changed the world* (pp. 34-36). New York: Viking.

Ebersole, Christine

Barr, N. (as told to). (2007, June). Christine Ebersole's aha! moment. *O, The Oprah Magazine, 8*(6). Retrieved from http://www.oprah.com/omagazine.html

Christine Ebersole. (n.d.). *Encyclopedia of World Biography*. Retrieved from http://www.notablebiographies.com/

Entekhabi-Fard, Camelia

Camelia Entekhabi-Fard's aha! moment. (2006, March). *O, The Oprah Magazine, 7*(3). Retrieved from http://www. oprah.com/omagazine.html

Entekhabifard, C. (2007). *Camelia: Save yourself by telling the truth—a memoir of Iran*. New York: Seven Stories Press.

Ephron, Nora

Ephron, N. (2006). *I Feel Bad About My Neck: And other thoughts on being a woman*. New York: Alfred A. Knopf.

Nora Ephron's aha! moment: At a crowded, chaotic screening, the Bewitched director learned a bit of magic. (2005, July). *O, The Oprah Magazine, 6*(7). Retrieved from http://www.oprah.com/omagazine.html

Falco, Edie

Colón, S. (as told to). (2009, June). Edie Falco's aha! moment. *O, The Oprah Magazine, 10*(6). Retrieved from http://www.oprah.com/omagazine.html

Fischer, Jenna

Bertsche, R. (as told to). (2007, May). Jenna Fischer's aha! moment. *O, The Oprah Magazine, 8*(5). Retrieved from http://www.oprah.com/omagazine.html

Friedman, Bonnie

Bonnie Friedman's aha! moment: "This is it my pet pachoch!". (2006, March). *O, The Oprah Magazine, 7*(3). Retrieved from http://www.oprah.com/omagazine.html

Friedman, B. (2002). *The Thief of Happiness: The story of an extraordinary psychotherapy.* Boston: Beacon Press.

Giovanni, Nikki

Barr, N. (as told to). (2007, September). Nikki Giovanni's aha! moment. *O, The Oprah Magazine, 8*(9). Retrieved from http://www.oprah.com/omagazine.html

Fowler, V.C. (1992). Interview with Nikki Giovanni [transcript of interview]. In V. C. Fowler (Ed.), *Conversations with Nikki Giovanni* (pp. 198-214).

Nikki Giovanni. (n.d.). *Poetry Foundation.* Retrieved from http://www.poetryfoundation.org/bio/nikki-giovanni

Nikki Giovanni: Bio—timeline. (n.d.). Retrieved from http://nikki-giovanni.com/timeline.shtml

Smith, T. (1992). Public radio book show: Nikki Giovanni [radio broadcast transcript]. In V. C. Fowler (Ed.), *Conversations with Nikki Giovanni* (pp. 188-197).

Goolagong, Evonne

Pearlman, J. (1998, May 25). Catching up with...Evonne Goolagong, tennis champion: April 26, 1976. *Sports Illustrated, 88*(21). Retrieved from http://sportsillustrated.cnn.com/features/1998/weekly/catchingup/0525/

Greene, Janice Schnake (See Schnake Greene, Janice)

Groban, Josh

Josh Groban's aha! moment. (2007, January). *O, The Oprah Magazine, 8*(1). Retrieved from http://www.oprah.com/omagazine.html

Hadden, Julie

All about Julie: Bio. (n.d.). Retrieved from http://www.juliehadden.com/

Hadden, J. (2009). *Fat Chance: Losing the weight, gaining my worth* [NOOK Book version]. Retrieved from www.barnesandnoble.com

Hadden, J. (n.d.). Worth the Weight. In *Paths to Happiness: 7 real life stories of personal growth, self-improvement and positive change* (pp. 5-8). Retrieved from http://www.guideposts.org (Original work published January 2009: *Guideposts, 63*(11), 42-46.)

julieb14. (2009, December 3). Fat chance: Losing the weight, gaining my worth [Web log post]. Retrieved from http://juliehaddenblog.wordpress.com/

Hamilton, Josh

Hamilton, J. (n.d.). "The Natural" plays again: The Texan Rangers outfielder John Hamilton on finding faith, bouncing back and holding on to hope to overcome his drug abuse. Retrieved from http://www.guideposts.org (Original work published July 2009: The natural. *Guideposts, 64*(5), 38-43.)

Hamilton, J. (with Keown, T.). (2008). *Beyond Belief: Finding the strength to come back.* New York: Hatchette Book Group.

Smallwood, J. (2010, October 27). Admire Rangers' Hamilton's story for what it is—one of salvation. philly.com. Retrieved from http://articles.philly.com/2010-10-27/sports/24952740_1_rangers-hamilton-roy-hobbs-drug-and-alcohol-abuse

Hamm, Mia

Currie, S. (2003). *Mia Hamm.* San Diego: Kidhaven Press.

Mia Hamm biography. (n.d.). *bio.* Retrieved from http://www.biography.com

Mia Hamm's aha! moment. (2004, August). *O, The Oprah Magazine, 5*(8). Retrieved from http://www.oprah.com/omagazine.html

Harden, Marcia Gay (2 insights)

Colón, S. (as told to). (2009, October). Maria Gay Harden's aha! moment. *O, The Oprah Magazine, 10*(10). Retrieved from http://www.oprah.com/omagazine.html

Harden, M. G. (n.d.). My best role ever: The inspiring story of how playing Snow White for a sick child changed Marcia Gay Harden's career. Retrieved from http://www.guideposts.org (Original work published March 2008: *Guideposts, 62*(13), 41-45.)

Marcia Gay Harden. (n.d.). *The New York Times.* Retrieved from http://movies.nytimes.com/person/30312/Marcia-Gay-Harden/biography

Marcia Gay Harden encourages graduates to cherish joys of life [Web log post]. (2010, May 24). *The University of Texas at Austin.* Retrieved from http://www.utexas.edu

Hirshberg, Gary

Hirshberg, G. (2008). *Stirring It Up: How to make money and save the world.* New York: Hyperion.

Hirshberg, G. (2008, February 25). "Seven cows and a dream". *Newsweek, 151*(8), E06.

Hirshberg, M. C. (2008, September). Hitched to someone else's dream. *Inc., 30*(9), 218-224.

Hutton, Timothy

Bertsche, R. (as told to). (2009, January). Timothy Hutton's aha! moment. *O, The Oprah Magazine, 10*(1). Retrieved from http://www.oprah.com/omagazine.html

Iman

Iman's aha! moment. (2002, October). *O, The Oprah Magazine, 3*(10). Retrieved from http://www.oprah.com/omagazine.html

"My brush with death"; Close calls changed perceptions and careers of notables. (1989, May). *Ebony, 44*(7), 96-100. Retrieved from http://books.google.com

Jemison, Mae

Mae Jemison's aha! moment. (2002, June). *O, The Oprah Magazine, 3*(6). Retrieved from http://www.oprah.com/omagazine.html

Jens, Kelly

Alexander, A. (2000). *Win the Fat War: 145 real-life secrets to weight-loss success.* Emmaus, PA: Rodale.

Robertson, S. (2001, November 13). A fit mother: Losing weight helps one mom be more involved in her kids' lives. *The Buffalo News*, p. C3.

Judd, Diana (See Judd, Naomi)

Judd, Naomi

Biography: About Naomi. (n.d.). Retrieved from www. naomijudd.com

Judd, N. (2004). *Naomi's Breakthrough Guide: 20 choices to transform your life.* New York: Simon & Schuster Paperbacks.

Judd, N. (with Schaetzle, B.). (1993). *Love Can Build a Bridge.* New York: Villard Books.

Keel, B. (2004, February 8). Sharing life lessons: Through the highs and lows of Naomi Judd's life, she's learned many things, but most importantly she's learned to be true to herself. *American Profile*, pp. 6-8.

Naomi Judd: Biography. (n.d.). *Academy of Achievement.* Retrieved from http://www.achievement.org/

Kanakaredes, Melina

10 Questions: Melina Kanakaredes. (n.d.). *DisneyFamily. com.* Retrieved from http://family.go.com/

Clawson, K. (2007, March 31). Temo's candy is an Easter tradition in Akron—Family has hand-dipped its chocolate at landmark on West Exchange since relocating there in 1947. *Akron Beacon Journal*, D1.

Melina Kanakaredes's aha! moment. (2001, February). *O, The Oprah Magazine, 2*(2). Retrieved from http://www.oprah.com/omagazine.html

Keoghan, Phil (2 insights)

Alter, E. (2004, October 5). Life lessons from Dr. Phil (Keoghan). *TV Guide.* Retrieved from http://www.tvguide.com/news/host-keoghan-race-42008.aspx#comments

Brooks, R. (2010, February). Pushing the envelope: A near-death experience in his teens enables the Amazing Race's Phil Keoghan to use fear for good. *Success,* 60+.

Keoghan, P. (with Berger, W.). (2004). *No Opportunity Wasted: 8 ways to create a list for the life you want.* Emmaus, PA: Rodale.

Keoghan, P. (2009, September). My amazing race: For the host of this hit TV show, life really *is* an incredible adventure. *Guideposts, 64*(7), 42-46.

Melton, M. (2009, October). Buzz: Encounter. *Los Angeles Magazine*, 38-40.

Klopfenstein, Pamela

Klopfenstein, P. (2010, January/February). A family affair: How they let another child into their lives, and their hearts. *Angels on Earth, 15*(3), 42-46.

Latifah, Queen (See Owens, Dana)

Lennox, Annie

Annie Lennox: Why I am an HIV/AIDS activist [Web video post]. (2010, September). *TED.* Retrieved from http://www.ted.com

Biography. (n.d.). Retrieved from http://www.annie-lennox.com/home.htm

van der Leun, J. (as told to). (2009, February). Annie Lennox's aha! moment. *O, The Oprah Magazine, 10*(2). Retrieved from http://www.oprah.com/omagazine.html

Leno, Jay

Aha! moments. (2006, March). *O, The Oprah Magazine, 7*(3). Retrieved from http://www.oprah.com/omagazine.html

Louis-Dreyfus, Julia

Smiley, T. (Interviewer). (2008, October 27). Julia Louis-Dreyfus [transcript of broadcast interview]. *pbs*. Retrieved from http://www.pbs.org/

Julia Louis-Dreyfus's aha! moment. (2006, May). *O, The Oprah Magazine, 7*(5). Retrieved from http://www.oprah.com/omagazine.html

Freydkin, D. (2008, April 22). The eco-adventures of Julia Louis-Dreyfus and Kate Hudson. *USA Today*. Retrieved from www.usatoday.com

Mac, Bernie (2 insights)

Frampton, S. (as told to). (2007, April). Bernie Mac's aha! moment. *O, The Oprah Magazine, 8*(4). Retrieved from http://www.oprah.com/omagazine.html

Mac, B. (with Dawsey, D.). (2001). *I Ain't Scared of You: Bernie Mac on how life is*. New York: Pocket Books.

Mandela, Nelson

The life and times of Nelson Mandela: Biography. (n.d.). Retrieved from http://www.nelsonmandela.org/

Mandela, N. (1994). *Long Walk to Freedom: The autobiography of Nelson Mandela*. Boston: Little, Brown and Company.

Mandela, N. (2010). *Conversations with Myself*. New York: Farrar, Straus, & Giroux.

Nelson Mandela—Biography. (n.d.). *Nobelprize.org*. Retrieved from http://www.nobelprize.org/

Margulies, Julianna

Capo-Garcia, P. (2008, July 22). "City Island" begins shooting. *Variety*. Retrieved from http://www.variety.com

Colón, S. (as told to). (2009, November). Julianna Margulies' aha! moment. *O, The Oprah Magazine, 10*(11). Retrieved from http://www.oprah.com/omagazine.html

Moore, F. (2008, March 11). Julianna Margulies plays it tough in "Canterbury's Law". AOL entertainment—Canada. Retrieved from http://entertainment.aol.ca/article/julianna-margulies-canterbury/148443/

Midler, Bette

van der Leun, J. (as told to). (2008, February). Bette Midler's aha! moment. *O, The Oprah Magazine, 9*(2). Retrieved from http://www.oprah.com/omagazine.html

Moore, Mary Tyler (See Tyler Moore, Mary)

Nixon, Cynthia

Nixon, C. (as told to Barr, N.). (2008, June). Aha! moment. *The Oprah Magazine, 9*(6). Retrieved from http://www.oprah.com/omagazine.html

Tallmer, J. (2009, March 18-24). Cynthia Nixon brings focus to "Distracted": Actress recalls early career, weighs in on Ritalin. *The Villager, 78*(41). Retrieved from http://www.thevillager.com/villager_307/cynthianixon.html

Silverman, S. M. (2008, April 16). Cynthia Nixon's latest role: Breast cancer advocate—and survivor. *People.* Retrieved from http://www.people.com/people/

Oh, Sandra

Sandra Oh's aha! moment. (2005, December). *The Oprah Magazine, 6*(12). Retrieved from http://www.oprah.com/omagazine.html

Orman, Suze

Orman, S. (2002). *Suze Orman's Financial Guidebook: Put the 9 steps to work.* New York: Three Rivers Press.

Orman, S. (2004). *The Laws of Money: 5 timeless secrets to get out and stay out of financial trouble.* New York: Free Press.

Orman, S. (2009, September). Suze Orman: "What money has taught me about personal power". *O, The Oprah Magazine, 10*(9). Retrieved from http://www.oprah.com/omagazine.html

Owens, Dana

Bertsche, R. (as told to). (2007, July). Queen Latifah's aha! moment. *O, The Oprah Magazine, 8*(7). Retrieved from http://www.oprah.com/omagazine.html

Parks, Suzan-Lori

Suzan-Lori Parks's aha! moment. (2003, May). *O, The Oprah Magazine, 4*(5). Retrieved from http://www.oprah.com/omagazine.html

Peale, Norman Vincent

George, C. V. R. (1993). *God's Salesman: Norman Vincent Peale and the power of positive thinking.* New York: Oxford University Press.

Peale, N. V. (1978). *The Power of Positive Thinking* (Special Peale Center edition). Pawling, NY: Peale Center for Christian Living.

Peale, N.V. (1984). *The True Joy of Positive Living: An autobiography.* New York: Morrow.

Takahama, V. (2002, April 14). The "Power of Positive Thinking" lives on. The *Buffalo News*, pp. E1, E3. (Reprinted from Positively 50: Norman Vincent Peale's powerful message still resonates a half century after it swept the country in *The Orange County Register*, pp. E1, E3, 2002, March 25.)

Peete, Holly Robinson (See Robinson Peete, Holly)

Pennington, Ty

Pennington, T. (n.d.). A career in changing lives. *Guideposts.* Retrieved from http://www.guideposts.org (Original work published August 2008: Design for life. *Guideposts, 63*(6), 26-31.)

Phillips, Nathan

Kwiatkowski, J. (2011, January 8). 375 pounds lighter. *The Buffalo News*, pp. C1-C2.

Procter, Emily

Procter, E. (2010, August). "What inspires me": A man named Jim and a cat named Kevin. *Guideposts, 65*(6), 40-43.

Queen Latifah (See Owens, Dana.)

Ralph, Sheryl Lee

Sheryl Lee Ralph's aha! moment. (2003, February). *O, The Oprah Magazine, 4*(2). Retrieved from http://www.oprah.com/omagazine.html

Rees, Bill

Gismondi, M. (2000). Dr. William Rees interviewed by D. Michael Gismondi. *Aurora Online*. Retrieved from http://aurora.icaap.org/index.php/aurora/index

Jones, D. (2005, October 10). Taking measure. *Time Canada, 166*(15), 50.

Rhimes, Shonda

Shonda Rhimes's aha! moment. (2006, March). *O, The Oprah Magazine, 7*(3). Retrieved from http://www.oprah.com/omagazine.html

Robinson Peete, Holly

Holly Robinson Peete's aha! moment. (2003, September). *O, The Oprah Magazine, 4*(9). Retrieved from http://www.oprah.com/omagazine.html

Rodham Clinton, Hillary (See Clinton, Hillary Rodham)

Romano, Michael

Romano, M. (2010, August 24). The defining moment: When I became a chef. *The Atlantic*. Retrieved from http://www.theatlantic.com/

Libby, B. (2001, December 18). Michael Romano: One of New York's top chefs talks about cooking on Sept. 11, kitchen piracy and why food shouldn't be an intellectual experience. *Salon*. Retrieved from http://www.salon.com/2001/12/18/romano/

Rose, Anika Noni

Martin, C. G. (as told to). (2009, December). Anika Noni Rose's aha! moment. *O, The Oprah Magazine, 10*(12). Retrieved from http://www.oprah.com/omagazine.html

Rosenberg Daniels, Cecelia

Broydo, L. (1999, October). The age of work. *Working Woman, 24*(9), 54-59.

Rossellini, Isabella

Archer, G. (2009, September 22). Isabella Rossellini frolics with *Green Porno* but there's a deeper message. *The Huffington Post.* Retrieved from http://www.huffingtonpost.com/

Medley, M. (2010, March 2). Isabella Rossellini's insatiable curiosity: Following her passion and her curiosity. *Success.* Retrieved from http://www.success.com/

Schneller, J. (as told to). (2009, September). Isabella Rossellini's aha! moment. *O, The Oprah Magazine, 10*(9). Retrieved from http://www.oprah.com/omagazine.html

Russert, Tim

Russert, T. (2004). *Big Russ and Me: Father and son, lessons of life.* New York: Miramax Books.

Tim Russert's aha! moment. (2005, January). *O, The Oprah Magazine, 6*(1). Retrieved from http://www.oprah.com/omagazine.html

Schnake Greene, Janice

Janice Schnake Greene. (n.d.). *Missouri State University.* Retrieved from http://www.missouristate.edu/

Lininger, G. (2010, March 16). Outstanding lifetime environmental education service award. *Missouri State University.* Retrieved from http://www.missouristate.edu/

Schnake Greene, J. (2010, March). Out of bounds. *Guideposts, 65*(1), 48-52.

Scott, Jill

Colón, S. (as told to). (2009, March). Jill Scott's aha! moment. *O, The Oprah Magazine, 10*(3). Retrieved from http://www.oprah.com/omagazine.html

Sedgwick, Kyra

Bertsche, R. (as told to). (2008, July). Kyra Sedgwick's aha! moment. *O, The Oprah Magazine, 9*(7). Retrieved from http://www.oprah.com/omagazine.html

Shriver, Maria (2 insights)

Shriver, M. (2008). *Just Who Will You Be?: Big question, little book, answers within.* New York: Hyperion.

Wolf, R. (2011, January 19). Sargent Shriver, first Peace Corps director, dies. *USA Today.* Retrieved from http://www.usatoday.com/

Smith, Dayna

Family room: Meet the people in our pages. (2010, July). *Guideposts, 65*(5), 79-82.

Smith, D. (2010, July). Not me. *Guideposts, 65*(5), 50-52.

Stone, Curtis

Mott, A. (2009, June). Cookbook. *House Beautiful, 151*(6), 52-55.

Styler, Trudie

Day, E. (2009, March 21). Trudie Styler: Why I had to use my celebrity to try to save the rainforest. *The Guardian.* Retrieved from http://www.guardiannews.com/

Hoggard, L. (2006, August 5). Trudie Styler: The truth about Trudie. *The Independent.* Retrieved from http://www.independent.co.uk/news/people/profiles/trudie-styler-the-truth-about-trudie-410523.html

Trudie Styler's aha! moment. (2002, March 15). *O, The Oprah Magazine.* Retrieved from http://www.oprah.com/omagazine.html

Sykes, Wanda

Wanda Sykes's aha! moment. (2003, November). *O, The Oprah Magazine, 4*(11). Retrieved from http://www.oprah.com/omagazine.html

Tolle, Eckhart

Tolle, E. (1997). *The Power of Now: A guide to spiritual enlightenment.* Novato, CA: New World Library.

Turlington, Christy

Christy Turlington's aha! moment. (2001, July). *O, The Oprah Magazine, 2*(7). Retrieved from http://www.oprah.com/omagazine.html

Tyler Moore, Mary

Mary Tyler Moore's aha! moment. (2006, April). *O, The Oprah Magazine, 7*(4). Retrieved from http://www.oprah.com/omagazine.html

Tyler Moore, M. (1995). *After All.* New York: G. P. Putnam's Sons.

Underwood, Blair

van der Leun, J. (as told to). (2008, November). Blair Underwood's aha! moment. *O, The Oprah Magazine, 9*(11). Retrieved from http://www.oprah.com/omagazine.html

Ward, Sela

Sela Ward's aha! moment. (2004, May). *O, The Oprah Magazine, 5*(5). Retrieved from http://www.oprah.com/omagazine.html

Ward, S. (2002). *Homesick: A memoir.* New York: ReganBooks.

Ward, S. (n.d.). Hope Village: Actress Sela Ward shares her inspiring story of creating a safe place for children. *Guideposts.* Retrieved from http://www.guideposts.org/ (Original work published December 2006: Bless the children. *Guideposts, 61*(10), 31-34.)

Washington, Kerry

Kerry Washington: Bio. (n.d.). *US Weekly.* Retrieved from http://www.usmagazine.com/celebrities

Kerry Washington's aha! moment. (2004, October). *O, The Oprah Magazine, 5*(10). Retrieved from http://www.oprah.com/omagazine.html

Watson, Karen

New firm helps pros achieve life balance. (2005, April 11). *San Diego Business Journal*, p. 20.

Wilder, Gene

Gene Wilder's aha! moment. (2005, March). *O, The Oprah Magazine, 6*(3). Retrieved from http://www.oprah.com/omagazine.html

Wilder, G. (2005). *Kiss Me Like a Stranger: My search for love and art.* New York: St. Martin's Press.

Wilson, Chandra

Bertsche, R. (as told to). (2008, March). Chandra Wilson's aha! moment. *O, The Oprah Magazine, 9*(3). Retrieved from http://www.oprah.com/omagazine.html

Woodard, Alfre

Alfre Woodard says she doesn't fit Hollywood's standards on beauty. (1999, January 11). *Jet, 95*(6), 62. Retrieved from http://books.google.com

Alfre Woodard's aha! moment. (2005, April). *O, The Oprah Magazine, 6*(4). Retrieved from http://www.oprah.com/omagazine.html

AHA! Index

Acknowledgements

How can I express my gratitude to all the people who have been instrumental in making this book a reality? I'm not sure that I have the words, but I will try.

My most heartfelt appreciation goes to David Hartney, Sallie Randolph, and Fran Ritzenthaler. David for your unwavering love, encouragement, and patience—not to mention your tireless review of and incisive input on each successive draft of the manuscript. Sallie for your boundless expertise and unending generosity. And, Fran for your unflagging enthusiasm for our work together and your support at every step along the way.

I am also grateful to the many people who read the manuscript at some point in its evolution and provided feedback and encouragement—Patti Baechler, Elise Ballard, Jenny Blake, Betsy Dechert-Boss, Cheryl Chambers, Dana Carter, Rosanne Dee, Jacqueline Dombrowski, Geri Grossman, Langdon Hubbard, Paul Kielich, Sharon Lucius, John McBride, Scott Stockton, Bob Strassburg, and Machelle Williams. Thank you.

Thank you to Cindy Kiple for your design vision, Sandy Beckwith for your publicity savvy, and Ronni Price for your social media know-how.

And thank you to those who have shared their experiences of life-changing AHA!s through articles, books, speeches, and other published accounts. Without those stories there would be no study, and no book.

About the Author

Author photograph © Mark Bennington

Donna Hartney, Ph.D., is an expert in life-changing insights. A rare combination of researcher, instructor, and case study, she is a performance consultant who works with global leaders and professionals at Fortune 500 companies. Hartney earned her Ph.D. from the University of North Carolina at Chapel Hill and lives with her family in Western New York. For more information, visit www.donnahartney.com.

CPSIA information can be obtained at www.ICGtesting.com
Printed in the USA
BVOW021800081112

305064BV00003B/2/P

9 780982 132814